The Rebuilding of Bosnia

Look for these and other books in the Lucent Overview Series:

The Rebuilding
of Bosnia

by James P. Reger

WORLD IN CONFLICT

LUCENT *Overview Series*

LUCENT Overview Series

Library of Congress Cataloging-in-Publication Data

Reger, James P.
    The rebuilding of Bosnia / by James P. Reger.
        p.   cm. — (Lucent overview series)
    Includes bibliographical references and index.
    Summary: Discusses the origins of the conflict in Bosnia and
efforts being made to bring peace to the area.
    ISBN 1-56006-190-1 (alk. paper)
    1. Yugoslav War, 1991– —Bosnia and Hercegovina—Juvenile
literature.   2. Bosnia and Hercegovina—History—Juvenile
literature.   [1. Yugoslav War, 1991– —Bosnia and Hercegovina.
2. Bosnia and Hercegovina—History.]   I. Title.   II. Series.
DR1313.3.R43   1997
949.703—dc21   96-29638
                                                                         CIP
                                                                          AC

Copyright © 1997 by Lucent Books, Inc.
P.O. Box 289011, San Diego, CA 92198-9011
Printed in the U.S.A.

Contents

Introduction

IN THE LATE 1980s, Yugoslavians Bosko Brckic and Admira Idmic were very much like any other teenagers in the Western world. They loved rock-and-roll music, dancing till dawn, fast cars, blue jeans, and each other. If anything might have set them apart from the majority of other young lovers, it was that they came from two different ethnic backgrounds. Bosko was a Serbian Orthodox boy and Admira was a Bosnian Muslim girl. But even that could not disrupt the passion reflected in their love letters.

"My dearest Admira," Bosko wrote when drafted into the Serb-dominated Yugoslav People's Army. "Every night when I go to bed I cannot sleep because I am thinking of you. My love, you are the only happiness I have."

Admira replied, "Just a little beat of time is left until we are together again and then absolutely nothing will separate us."

"My dearest Admira," Bosko wrote back, "truly I miss you so much that I cannot say or express it in words. Now all my life points to the day when I will finish my military service and see you again at home in Sarajevo."

Clearly, there was no thought here of racial "purity" or "ethnic cleansing." Sarajevo, Bosnia, was, after all, a multi-ethnic conglomeration of Serbian Orthodox, Bosnian Muslim, and Croatian Roman Catholic citizens, and it seemed to foster the success of "mixed" relationships. Indeed, since Yugoslav Communist leader Marshal Tito's suppression of ethnic nationalism after World War II, more than 25 percent of all Balkan marriages were mixed. The percentage was closer to 35 percent in cosmopolitan Sarajevo.

When Tito's away the mice will play

In 1991, eleven years after Tito's death, forty-five years of sublimated nationalistic and religious tensions erupted and Yugoslavia's ethnic communities began to agitate. The Roman Catholic republics of Slovenia and Croatia, and, later, Muslim Bosnia declared their independence from the Serbian-dominated Yugoslav federal government. The Orthodox Serbs attempted to keep the nation together by force, but they had no luck at all against the Slovenians and found it tough going against the Croats. But Bosnia turned out to be a different matter.

Since there were so many Serbs already living in Bosnia and Bosnia was militarily weak—Serbia had inherited most of federal Yugoslavia's weaponry—the Serbian forces were able to quickly surround and lay siege to the Bosnian capital of Sarajevo. The Serbs had decided that this symbol of internationalism and tolerance had to be destroyed before it could be saved.

In Sarajevo, a man walks amidst the ruins of apartment buildings after Serbian forces besieged the Yugoslavian capital.

The breakout

The effect on Bosko and Admira was devastating. As the Muslim death toll mounted at the hands of the besieging Serbs, Bosko, himself a Serb, emerged as an easy target for the frustrated Muslims who dominated Sarajevo. They threatened his life with increasing vehemence until it became clear that he would have to escape to the Serbian side.

Admira insisted upon accompanying her lover, fully aware of the risks involved in attempting to cross the bullet-raked no-man's-land between the two lines and the bitterness she, as a Muslim, would encounter on the other side. "It's better for us to be together," she told her mother, "no matter what will happen." Her mother said through her farewell tears, "Truly, there has never been a love as great as yours."

Crosses in a Sarajevo cemetery mark the graves of those killed during the war in Bosnia. Tens of thousands of Bosnians, Serbs, and Croats lost their lives during the fighting.

Bosko and Admira assured their parents that everything would be fine. They told them that they had arranged for a short truce at a bridge crossing through a Muslim friend with reliable connections and they trusted that he would not let them down. They were so confident, in fact, that they were skipping hand in hand as they approached the bridge. But something went wrong, terribly wrong. Rifles

opened up. Bosko spasmed to the ground instantly, a bullet through his head. Screaming from the agony of her own mortal wounds, Admira crawled over and cradled him in her arms. And then they died as they had lived, together in a loving embrace, leaving a suffocating silence and a pool of ethnically mixed blood.

"Oh, my God," Bosko's mother cried, upon seeing the two bodies on the television news. "Is it possible that this could be happening again in this century? They died for each other. Even now, in my mind, I can see them hugging each other and laughing." And she dropped her sobbing face into her hands.

Wars end/pain doesn't

For another week the world television audience watched the bodies bloat on the evening news. It took that long for the warring parties to sufficiently deny responsibility for the killings and agree on a burial truce. Admira's father, strangely compelled to watch, could only say, "I still can't believe they are dead; that all their plans, their wishes, were sunk after one bullet, one burst, one monstrous act. That is proof that love cannot conquer all. Love cannot win over people who do not believe in love."

A year after the killings, Admira's mother still had to fight back tears to say, "We are hoping that something will change and that the madness will stop. There must be an end to all of this. I don't know how long it will take. But someday it has to stop."

And it did stop after three more brutal years, thousands more atrocities, tens of thousands more deaths, and hundreds of thousands more "ethnically cleansed" refugees. But what brought on this madness in the first place? How could a people who originally had so much in common have ever come to treat each other with such barbarity? And more importantly, what is to keep those same hostilities from erupting again and again as Bosnia and the other former Yugoslav republics struggle to establish their new and diverging identities? As is so often the case, an understanding of the present is dependent upon an understanding of the past.

1

A Long, Rocky Road to War

THE EARLIEST SEEDS of dissent took root in the Balkans long before the Slavic Serbs, Croats, and Bosnians even lived there. In A.D. 395 the Christian Church schismed (divided) into the Eastern Orthodox, or Byzantine, and the Roman Catholic Churches, splitting the mountainous region right down the middle. The Roman Catholics claimed the northern Balkans and the Eastern Orthodox took the southern ones. When the ancestors of the modern Slavs began migrating into these lands from northeastern Europe and Ukraine around A.D. 500, they adopted one religion or the other depending upon where they settled, thereby establishing the first of what would become many critical disparities.

Tribal enmities

The religions themselves created further distinctions in dialects, alphabets, and customs. The Roman Catholics introduced the northern Croats and Slovenians to the Roman alphabet while the southern Serbs picked up the Greek-influenced Cyrillic alphabet, thereby inhibiting communication between them. Different interpretations of Christian scripture also led to the divergence of worship practices and doctrines. Soon the Catholic and Orthodox Slavs saw each other as practitioners of devil-bred heresy.

The jagged, mountainous terrain also weakened the connective bonds that had previously linked Slavs. The steep cliffs, wide rivers, and narrow valleys rendered travel difficult and defense easy, reinforcing each tribe's sense of isolation and separateness. Increasingly, when different groups did have contact, it was to compete for the precious little flat, arable land. These contacts often led to killings that cried out for revenge and eventually sparked tribal warfare.

Split by holy empires

From approximately A.D. 1400 on, intra-Slavic aggression was exacerbated by an even greater peril: invasion and occupation by foreign empires. Hungary and later Austria-Hungary conquered Croatia (and neighboring Slovenia) while the Ottoman Turks took over Bosnia and Serbia. As a result, Croatia fell under the sphere of Roman Catholic Europe, especially Austria-Hungary and Germany, and developed

Ottoman Turks capture the eastern city of Constantinople in 1453. During the fifteenth century, Ottoman Turks expanded their empire by conquering other empires and countries, including Bosnia and Serbia.

stronger ties to the West. Bosnia and Serbia, on the other hand, were forced under the dominion of the East with bonds to Turkey and, later, peasant Russia.

Serbia's greatest national heroes and patriotic legends spring from this era and fuel their respect for warriors even today. None inspire them to acts of defiance, vengeance, and fervent nationalism more than those described here by a contemporary Balkan historian:

> Between June 5 and 28, 1389, on the Field of Blackbirds, now known as Kosovo, the rebelling forces of Serbia were soundly defeated by the advancing Turkish armies of Sultan Murad I. Murad I himself was assassinated in Kosovo soon after the first battle [some accounts say by Serbian king Lazar himself after he feigned surrender]. His son, who became the Sultan Bayazid, was also with the Turkish armies in the Balkans. He immediately ordered the execution of the captive king as a blood revenge. Meanwhile, the Turkish armies intensified their assault on the remaining Serbian forces. Consequently, by June 28, 1389, the land of the Yugo Slavs [southern Slavs] was completely occupied by the Muslim Turks, and so began the centuries-long struggle of the southern Slavs, led by the Serbs, for independence and self-determination.

Some Slavs bore the yoke of imperialism more agreeably than others. Croatia seemed almost eager to acquire the benefits of the West's cultural renaissance and developing industry. Bosnia and Serbia, however, remained in the Eastern peasant age with its subsistence farming and lack of technology. And they suffered another further dichotomy, this one within the Ottoman Empire.

An introduction to Islam

The Ottoman Turks introduced the Islamic faith to both communities. Bosnia accepted this new religion—and the Turkish promises of lower taxes for those who converted—while the Serbs clung fiercely to their Orthodox faith. According to the great writer/historian H. G. Wells, "The Ottomans converted what they could of the conquered people to Islam; the Serbian Christians they disarmed and conferred upon them the monopoly of

tax-paying." It was during the five oppressive centuries to come that many Serbians migrated into unpopulated areas of Bosnia and Croatia in search of tax relief.

During the nineteenth century, the Ottomans, weakened by rivalries with Britain, Russia, and Austria-Hungary, lost control of Serbia and Bosnia. The Serbs lived much of this century under their own Serbian monarchy. Bosnia fell into Austro-Hungarian (and thus Croat) hands by way of treaty in 1878. In July 1914 a Serbian assassinated Archduke Francis Ferdinand, the heir to the Austro-Hungarian throne. The assassin had hoped only to effect the transfer of Bosnia to his own country but, due to a series of convoluted European treaties, he started World War I instead.

In a rush to enlist, Serbian men flock to the war bureau in this 1914 photograph. During World War I, Serbia joined the Allies in their fight against Germany.

A failed attempt at nationhood

World War I in the Balkans saw the Slovenians, Croatians, and Bosnians allied with Germany against the Allied powers, including the United States, while Serbia fought with the Allies. Those four grisly years of assembly-line death led to the demise or the decline of every

German soldiers patrol the streets of a small Yugoslavian town on May 9, 1941. World War II brought civil war to the Balkans, pitting Croats, Serbs, and Communist Partisans against each other.

empire that had been competing for the Balkans. A treaty at the war's end created an entirely new country from the "free-floating" Slavic states called the Kingdom of the Serbs, Croats, and Slovenes. Ten years later a Serbian dictator, King Alexander, took over and changed the name of the country to Yugoslavia, meaning the "land of the southern Slavs." Alexander was soon assassinated by Croats wanting independence, but the name for the country stuck.

Alexander's son, Peter, tried to take over where his father had left off, but the artificially imposed nationhood never really took hold. With three distinct cultures and religions, conflict became inevitable and it broke out among the squabbling groups in the form of murders and reprisals. The ultimate unraveling of the nation came as no surprise to the Slavs themselves. They had distrusted each other for fifteen hundred years and not even the threat of common enemies had been able to unite them. In any attempted alliance, the question had always been the same: Who would have more power over whom? And they could never agree on that.

The "forgotten" holocaust

As Adolf Hitler's Nazi armies goose-stepped their way toward German domination over Europe in the 1930s and '40s, Yugoslavians could only bicker within their own fractious country. Serbians, boasting that they had the greatest population, land mass, and experience governing, claimed that they should hold the reins of leadership. The Bosnian Muslims, accepting their smaller numbers and weak military capability, were willing to trade their claims to power for the promise of religious tolerance. The Croatians, however, would not accept a Serb-dominated federal government. They finally gave up altogether and began to look for another route to sovereignty. That route seemed to auspiciously present itself when Hitler's Nazis headed south on their way to conquer the Greeks and outflank the Russians.

World War II in the Balkans broke down into two major killing grounds. The first encompassed a three-way civil war fought between combat troops and guerrilla raiders that, while unusually bitter, was at least waged with weapons in every participant's hands. The German-backed Croatians—the Ustaša—fought against Serb Royalist Chetniks as well as Communist Partisans under Tito. The Serbs and Communists raided the German-Croats and each other until the Communist Russians arrived to thwart both the Germans-Croats and the Serb Chetniks.

Wartime atrocities

At the end of the war, the Russians were in charge along with their proxies, the Communist Partisans. As they swept the defeated Nazis and Croatian Ustaša from power in the north, the second major killing ground revealed itself. This one had not been the result of "fair" fights with armed soldiers risking their lives to kill other armed soldiers. This was a collection of concentration camps where Croatians, with some help from the Bosnian Muslims, had murdered between 500,000 and 700,000 Croatian Serb and Bosnian Serb civilians.

There had been hideous tortures as well. A long-bearded Orthodox bishop and priest were

> shaved with a blunt knife. Their eyes were gouged out and their noses and ears cut off while a fire was lighted on their chests. Finally, when the Croat tormentors decided that their victims had suffered enough, they were given the coup de grace [death blow], which ended their agony.

The Croats threw thousands more screaming Serbs from steep, craggy cliffs, where their bodies burst open on the rocks below only to rot in the sun. Rivers were also another favorite spot for the Ustaša to dispose of bodies. At times the blood and muck of decaying corpses rendered the once-clear mountain waters unfit for human consumption.

One Serb who somehow survived the following atrocity reported, "Some 250 peasants, both men and women, were forced to dig a long trench in a field and then, with their hands tied behind their backs, they were buried alive in this tomb."

According to a French historian,

> The well-known industrialist and philanthropist, Serb Milos Teslic from Sisak [Croatia], was cruelly tortured and killed by Ustashi [Ustaša]. His legs were broken, ears and lips cut off, eyes gouged out, chest stabbed, and finally the heart was extracted through a big hole made in his chest. The Ustashi themselves said that the heart of the tortured Milos was still beating in the palm of the man who cut it out.

This May 6, 1941, photograph depicts Serbian prisoners of war after their capture by German forces. Some 500,000 to 700,000 Serbs were slaughtered in concentration camps during World War II.

Probing reports that the Balkan holocaust was originating with the top Croatian leadership, an Italian writer interviewed Croat president Ante Pavelić and reported:

> While he talked, I kept looking at a wicker basket placed on his desk. The lid was raised and in the basket was a variety of

Yugoslavia After World War II

seafood, or so it seemed. "Oysters from Dalmatia?" I inquired. Pavelić raised the lid of the basket higher and, showing me the sticky seafood that looked like a mass of sticky, gelatinous oysters, he said with a tired, kindly smile: "A gift from my loyal Ustashi. Forty pounds of Serbian eyeballs."

With atrocities such as these so recently committed upon their people, it is little wonder that the Serbs resisted being united with either the Croats or the Bosnian Muslims in post–World War II Yugoslavia. This time, however, it was the Russian chief Joseph Stalin and the Yugoslav Communist Partisan leader, Tito, who were exerting the external pressure and military might to make a single nation out of the Balkans.

This attempt at reunification proved to be a daunting one, but Tito, after separating Yugoslavia from the Soviet bloc in 1948, successfully, if harshly, imposed his creed of "Unity and Brotherhood" on all the nationalist hatreds. And for the thirty-five years of his dictatorship, relative peace prevailed. He died, though, in 1980, leaving no one behind him who could keep the contentious factions together.

2

The Flames of War Reignite

IN 1989 ONE man did step forward and try to hold Yugoslavia together in his own opportunistic way. His name was Slobodan Milošević, the newly elected president of the Serb Republic. He was driven by a personal quest for power that he hoped to manifest by uniting and controlling all Serbs living throughout the Balkans in what has been called "Greater Serbia."

When the other republics threatened to secede from Yugoslavia if he attempted such a move, Milošević declared that he would use military force to keep the nation together. Since he controlled the Serb-dominated Yugoslav National Army (the fourth largest in Europe), such threats had to be taken seriously.

The Kosovo example

Milošević devised a cunning strategy to mobilize the patriotic and honest Serbian people behind his personal power-grab. Using the government-controlled television, radio, and print media, he stirred up the fires of nationalism with a blitz of visions about the greatness of past Serbian heroes and the renewed threat of past enemies such as Croatia and Bosnia. He first brought his scheme to bear on a small southern corner of Serbia: the semiautonomous province of Kosovo. The Albanian majority there had been discussing independence for several months and Milošević decided to make an example of them.

All Serbian battlefields are holy to the Serbs and the holiest of holies is the Field of Blackbirds, where Serbian knights fell gloriously to the Ottoman Turks in A.D. 1389. Unfortunately for the Albanian-blooded Kosovans, that sacred battlefield happens to be located in their province, and after two years of Milošević's propaganda, the Serbs were not about to let it go.

As the other disgruntled republics looked on, Milošević sent in tanks and troops to put down strikes and protests. His army quickly crushed all resistance. At the huge, well-choreographed rally that followed at the Field of Blackbirds, Milošević crowed in victory

Through nationalism and military might, Serbian president Slobodan Milošević hoped to control all of Yugoslavia.

> This rally shows that no one can destroy the country because the people won't let them. The people are the best guarantee. We are going to get all the honest people in Yugoslavia to fight for peace and unity. Nothing can stop the Serb leadership and people from doing what we want!

The crowd of one million cheered until they were drunk with passion. Then President Milošević, always appreciative of symbolism and media images, ascended into the heavens in his helicopter and sped away to implement the next step in his plan.

Not much of a war

Slovenia, a Serbless province in the north, declared its secession from Milošević's Yugoslavia in the spring of 1991 and the European Union soon recognized their independence—against the wishes of U.S. president George Bush, who wanted to keep Yugoslavia whole. Milošević lost no time in ordering the Yugoslav National Army (the JNA) into action. A Yugoslav general, watching the tanks roll into Slovenia and hearing the staccato gunfire, remarked:

> I realized then that this was not a revolt or a political demonstration as in Kosovo, but that it was war. We realized that

In Croatia, refugees find shelter in a gymnasium after being forced to leave their homes. During the Serbian invasion, hordes of Croats were displaced from their homes and subjected to "ethnic cleansings."

they wanted to kill us, to shoot us, that there was no Yugoslavia and that there was no more life together with them.

Although the "war" only lasted ten days and caused comparatively few casualties, Milošević called off the fight and let Slovenia separate more or less peacefully. He found he had a far more serious crisis brewing in neighboring Croatia, where its president, Franjo Tudjman, was trying to pull that northern republic out of Yugoslavia (again with European but not U.S. recognition) and taking its persecuted 12 percent Serb minority with him against their will. This was too much for Milošević to bear. Finally, full-scale war exploded.

Croatia: A Serbian ending to World War II

With heavy tanks, long-range artillery, and jet airpower, the Yugoslav National Army along with Croatian Serb paramilitaries crashed into the eastern Croatian regions of Krajina and Slavonia and grabbed a wide arc of territory. There they commenced their first instances of "ethnic cleansing" in the name of "payback" for the atrocities of World War II. An English journalist present reported:

The Croatian cities were filling up with legions of the dispossessed: Croats who had been forcibly removed from their homes or had fled the Serb advance. Whole communities decamped overnight, carrying what could be carried, and leaving everything else behind to be looted or destroyed. Croatia's militia had been caught off guard and they were no match for the heavily-armed Serbs.

The war in Croatia, undeclared and dirty, reached its climax at a town called Vukovar when the JNA and Croatian Serb paramilitaries began what became a three-month siege. Hundreds of civilians were blasted to pieces by indiscriminate artillery fire from the hills ringing the town. When the Croatian Serb infantry finally took over the remains, many non-Serb military-age men were beaten, tortured, or murdered, just as Serbs had been in areas of recent Croatian cleansings.

The next two months of battle—with grisly casualties on both sides—brought several other Croatian cities to their knees, but after that Milošević stopped his advance. When his generals protested, he said simply, "We have no job there in Croat-populated areas. We have to protect the Serb areas only." It did not matter to Milošević that those "Serb areas" were lands that had belonged to Croatia for centuries.

A woman sullenly inspects the destruction of her neighbor's house after the Yugoslavia National Army (JNA) and Croatian Serb paramilitaries assaulted the Croatian town of Vukovar.

By January 1992 both sides had agreed to a cease-fire brokered by Cyrus Vance of the United Nations. With it, the Serbs would get to keep the conquered land on which the Croatian Serbs lived—one-third of Croatia—while fourteen thousand UN peacekeeping troops would separate the warring factions. And so ended the first, but by no means the worst, phase of the fighting.

Bosnia: Adrift in a sea of enemies

Serb-dominated or "Rump" Yugoslavia—this time with the help of the Bosnian Serbs—next brought its firepower

to bear on the latest province to declare its independence: Bosnia-Herzegovina, more commonly known as Bosnia.

Militarily weak and lacking a warrior tradition, Bosnia appeared to be an easy conquest. The JNA crossed the border, and the Bosnian Serbs, under the leadership of psychiatrist-turned-politician Radovan Karadzic, rose up from within the mountains of Bosnia. Together their tanks, infantry, and armored vehicles "cleansed" the Muslims and Croats out of many towns and cities. Muslim-populated Zvornik suffered one of the first takeovers and served as a model for many others.

An Italian diplomat who arrived in Zvornik just after the carnage said:

> I could see trucks full of dead bodies. I could see Bosnian Serb militiamen taking more corpses of children, women, and old people from their houses and putting them on trucks. I saw at least four or five trucks full of corpses. When I arrived, the cleansing had been done. There were no people, no

A soldier covers his face as he walks past recovered corpses found near Zvornik, where JNA and Bosnian Serbs went on a murderous rampage, massacring the town's Muslim population.

Muslim men are lodged in a refugee camp after being forced out of their homes. By December 1992, half of Bosnia's population had been either killed or relocated.

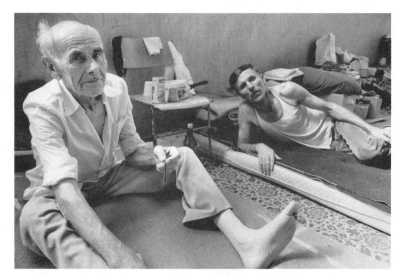

one on the streets. It was all finished. The militiamen were looting, cleaning up the city after the massacre.

The diplomat returned to the city months later and saw that it had been inhabited by Bosnian Serb families. Where the "cleansed" Muslim refugees had ended up, he did not know. Although, he had his suspicions.

Cleansing with a barbed-wire brush

Riding on the momentum of the victories in eastern Bosnia, the Bosnian and Rump Yugoslav Serbs drove the Bosnian Croats and Muslims from the "Posavina Corridor" in northern Bosnia. The Serbs sought this channel of land because it linked up Serbia proper with its newly won territory in eastern Croatia—Slavonia. They burned their way through the corridor with a brutal vengeance, cleansing record numbers of Muslim and Croat refugees. By December 1992 two million Bosnians—one-half of Bosnia's entire population—had been killed or relocated.

Most of the homeless victims ended up squatting in Croatian camps. The rest, thousands upon thousands of them, still needed places to stay and the Bosnian Serbs supplied them with "shelter." They herded the stray Muslims into prison camps, where one witness observed, "300 Muslim had been imprisoned in an ore loader inside a cage roughly 700 square feet. The cages were stacked four high and separated by grates. There were no toilets and the prisoners had to live in their own filth, which dripped through the grates."

Another said:

> The starving men are at various stages of human decay and affliction; the bones of their elbows and wrists protrude like pieces of jagged stone from the pencil-thin stalks to which their arms have been reduced. Their stares burn, they speak only with their terrified silence and eyes inflamed with the articulation of stark, undiluted, desolate fear-without-hope.

A 1993 report by the U.S. government to the United Nations cited, among other offenses, slit throats, suffocations, beatings, genital mutilations, rapes, dismemberment of heads, hands, and feet, cigarette burns, electric shocks, shootings, eyes gouged out, knifings, and prisoners being forced to run barefooted over broken glass and to drink caustic materials.

No angels/no heroes

It should be noted that all three sides in this war, the Serbs, Croats, and the Muslims, committed atrocities and did so approximately in proportion to their own numbers as well as to their opportunities to commit the heinous acts. Since the Serbs dominate the former Yugoslavia in terms of population and since their superior military capacity enabled them to take more prisoners, especially early in the war, it is not surprising that Karadzic's Bosnian Serb forces, under the command of General Ratko Mladic and sponsored by Slobodan Milošević, committed the majority of reported war crimes—between 65 to 90 percent depending upon the source.

This does not render the Serbs worse as individuals than the Muslims or Croats, who stepped up their atrocities toward the end of the war when their military advances provided them with greater opportunities to do so. It simply means that, in this extraordinarily bitter war, there were no angels and there were no heroes. There were only men whom circumstances too often stripped of their humanity.

And, of course, there were their victims. Regardless of the reason, however, all agree that Bosnia, in 1992, collapsed beneath the savagery of the largest and most brutal reign of terror since the cataclysm of World War II. It also witnessed the beginning of the war's longest and most notable battle: the three-year siege of Sarajevo.

A modern city in a dark age feud

Sarajevo stood for everything that most Serbs resented, especially those living in rural areas to whom the Sarajevans referred to as "primitive people." It was a sophisticated city with cosmopolitan ways and it had long since proven that many diverse cultures, races, and religions could peacefully and prosperously coexist. In 1984 its tolerance had received worldwide accolades when it hosted the international Winter Olympic Games. The Bosnian president, Muslim Alija Izetbegović, boasted of his capital's ethnic blend of 44 percent Muslim, 31 percent Orthodox Serb, and 17 percent Roman Catholic Croat while counting on its Muslim majority to keep him in power.

That blend separated out, though, in both the republic and the capital city when the Bosnian Serbs declared their

These women are part of a group of nearly five thousand women and children who fled to Croatia after Serbian forces laid siege to Sarajevo. Before the attack, Sarajevo boasted an ethnically mixed population that included Muslims, Orthodox Serbs, and Roman Catholic Croats.

own independent Serbian Republic of Bosnia with Karadzic as their president and largely drew its boundaries along ethnic lines. The early battling around Sarajevo and the indications that a siege would follow encouraged most of the city's Serbs to flee.

The siege began in April 1992 when the Serbs opened up their heavy artillery from the high mountains surrounding Sarajevo and from suburbs they had "cleansed" earlier. A river roughly separated the warring sides of the city, but it could not prevent the Serbs from blasting much of the twentieth-century high-rises into medieval rubble.

In war-torn Sarajevo, three young boys huddle on the ground after mortar shells fell close to where they were collecting firewood.

The Bosnian Muslims returned the fire as best they could but they were outgunned. Even when Milošević's Yugoslav National Army pulled out after a few months, they conspicuously left their tanks and heavy artillery in Bosnian Serb hands. The Bosnian Muslims eventually received weapons and soldiers from Iran and other Islamic countries, but not before ten thousand Sarajevan civilians had been killed. The following eyewitness account represents the results of one Serbian bombardment:

> Fourteen dead bodies were found in the school yard. Body parts clung to the school-yard fence. The ground was literally soaked with blood. One child, about six years of age, had been decapitated. I saw two ox-carts covered with bodies. I did not look forward to closing my eyes that night for fear that I would relive the images. I will never be able to convey the horror.

It's a mad, mad, mad, mad war

Animalistic fighting seared Bosnia for the next two years without anyone on any side really being able to understand all of its endless twists and nuances. What can be said generally is that the Muslim forces and civilians continued to lose ground—two-thirds of Bosnia-Herzegovina's original territory—to either the Croats or the Serbs, and they ended up crammed together in the center and a northwest pocket of Bosnia. The Bosnian Serbs took over a

Muslim refugees aboard UN transports prepare to evacuate Srebrenica after Bosnian Serbs stormed the "safe area," killing an estimated four thousand Muslims.

wide arc of northern and eastern Bosnia, and the Bosnian Croats conquered southwestern Bosnia.

However, many ironies contradicted the overall pattern. In Bihać (the northwest pocket), a large group of rebel Muslims took up arms against their own Islamic Bosnian government and allied with the Bosnian Croats and Serbs to fight Izetbegović's loyal Bosnian Muslims holding the city. In other areas of Bosnia, the UN peacekeepers militarily reinforced several cities as off-limit "safe areas" to provide protection for Muslim refugees, but the Bosnian Serbs overran them anyway and the outnumbered UN "Blue Helmets" could do nothing to stop it.

Bosnian Serbs, under the leadership of General Ratko Mladic, stormed one such "safe area," Srebrenica, and allegedly murdered over four thousand unarmed Muslim men. Mladic—considered by one diplomat to be a "psychopath"—claimed that he attacked in the first place because Muslim militiamen had staged raids on his Serbs from the "safe area." And the "psychopath" appears to have been telling the truth.

The ironies mounted as the fighting continued. UN relief supplies intended for surrounded Muslims at Sarajevo ended up being sold on the black market, making corrupt UN soldiers and Bosnian Muslim marketeers rich and all but the wealthiest buyers devoid of the essential supplies. A tap-water shortage that was blamed on the besieging Serbs and that necessitated Muslims having to risk sniper fire to get jugged water turned out to have been intentionally caused by the Muslim government itself in an effort to engender international sympathy. Also, for the length of the war, the international parties maintained an arms blockade on all the belligerent parties, in effect freezing the Serbian military superiority in place. The United States, who favored better arming of the Muslims, were said to have allowed their archenemy Iran and other militant Islamic countries to freely violate the blockade in hopes of balancing Izetbegović's forces with those of the Serbs.

Adding to the confusion, Bosnian Croats who had fought alongside the Muslims at the outset of the war flip-flopped their allegiances and fought against them for two years before realigning with the Muslims against the Serbs toward the end of the conflict. Tudjman's Croatians and Milošević's Serbs kept giving and then withdrawing their support for their respective Bosnian brothers, and dozens of cease-fires were agreed to and broken by all sides. The

In Bosnia, a young girl carries buckets of water through the snow. A tap-water shortage forced Bosnians to leave the safety of their homes to retrieve water for their families, thereby exposing themselves to deadly sniper fire.

"I dread to think what'll happen when the ceasefire ends!"

most vile irony of all, however, alleges that the Bosnian Muslims and their Iranian sponsors attempted to manipulate world opinion by blowing up scores of their own innocent civilians in a Sarajevo marketplace and then blaming the deaths on the Serbs. There is some evidence to suggest that they may have committed other similar outrages against their own people.

The end?

In 1995 the United States, the leading member of the North Atlantic Treaty Organization (NATO), finally became exasperated by the inability of the UN to stop the wanton killing. They and the European powers were close to pulling out of the Balkans altogether when the Serbs undeniably bombed and killed over thirty Sarajevan civilians in the same marketplace that had been mysteriously bombed a year earlier. At last provoked to full-scale intervention, NATO planes began bombing Bosnian Serb positions around Sarajevo and other threatened Muslim cities. The Serbs reacted by taking UN soldiers hostage and trading them for bomb-free skies. More bombs fell, however, but stopped again when the Serbs took more hostages. This cat-and-mouse game might have gone on longer, but the Muslims and Croats forged their final alliance and launched a successful offensive throughout Bosnia in the wake of the NATO airstrikes.

Word circulated of another attempted cease-fire and all sides intensified their hostilities, rushing to grab or hold on to as much territory as possible before they sat down to negotiate. The Croatian-Muslim alliance rallied a major push and drove 150,000 Serbs from Croatia and northwestern Bosnia in the largest cleansing of the entire war. For their part, the Serbs consolidated their gains in eastern Bosnia and scrambled to find camps for the mobs of Serbian refugees flooding toward Serbia proper.

Oddly, it would be this last Balkan hemorrhage that would pave the way for substantive peace talks. From the increased death and homeless misery, favorable circumstances for a settlement were about to unfold. And this time, it would be U.S. president Bill Clinton who would broker the deal.

3

A Treaty Forged in Dayton

SINCE AUGUST 1995, U.S. assistant secretary of state Richard Holbrooke had been shuttling between the capitals of all the major factions involved in the Bosnian catastrophe: Washington, D.C.; Belgrade, Yugoslavia (Serbia proper); Zagreb, Croatia; Sarajevo, Bosnia (Muslim Bosnia); Moscow in Russia; and back to Washington. He dealt with the Bosnian Serbs through Milošević's Rump Yugoslavia. Listening to every side's demands and demanding that they, too, listen, he hammered out deal after ever-evolving deal until he was approaching an agreement that looked like it might satisfy all the groups concerned.

With his boundless energy and competitive drive, Holbrooke refused to be bullied by the bullies. He demanded rather than debated, and he laid out a workable plan for the restructuring of Bosnia that, while not completely fair to everyone, at least promised to end the war with every side's original war aims being partially met.

Richard Holbrooke does not fit the mold of most diplomats, and he has garnered many enemies throughout his career as a result. One such detractor cited his "perpetual self-aggrandizement, his hyper-active ambition, his excessive energy, his hunger for public triumph, his stagy brilliance, and his bullying, beseeching ways." A friend countered by saying, "He's a son of a bitch, but he's our son of a bitch, which made him the perfect choice to manage a negotiation process featuring Serbian war criminals,

Croatian Reich-builders, and endlessly squabbling Muslims." And that is precisely why U.S. president Bill Clinton and secretary of state Warren Christopher gave him the daunting job negotiating an end to the war.

The players

In the early 1990s, after ten years of political drift without Tito, most of the former Yugoslav republics declared their independence and held their first democratic elections. Croats, Bosnians, and Serbs elected or otherwise empowered the men who would decide their futures, and they could not have chosen a more volatile group.

Acting as the mediator between the Croats, Serbs, and Muslims, U.S. assistant secretary of state Richard Holbrooke diligently negotiated an end to the war in Bosnia.

The last U.S. ambassador to Yugoslavia, Warren Zimmerman, knew them all well and described them variously. He said Bosnian president Alija Izetbegović was "mild-mannered, deferential, and perpetually anxious; he wore the mantle of leadership with great discomfort. A devout Muslim but no extremist, he had consistently advocated the preservation of a multinational Bosnia." Of the four leaders, Izetbegović may have most preferred peace to war initially, but after he allied with Iran and then Croatia, his heart hardened considerably.

By 1994, he had cultivated an ethic of vengeance within him as vitriolic as any of the Balkan leaders. His talk of peaceful coexistence had been replaced by such statements as, "We will use all means to get out of this misery, I want to stress: all means. And regarding the Serb criminals, I want to let them know that we will pay them back in kind, and very soon. That day is not far away!"

Ambassador Zimmerman referred to Croatian president Franjo Tudjman this way: "Tudjman resembles an inflexible school teacher. Prim steel eyeglasses hang on his square face, whose natural expression is a scowl. His mouth occasionally creases into a nervous chuckle or

Bosnian president Alija Izetbegović waves to crowds during a military parade. Izetbegović originally advocated keeping Bosnia multinational; however, as the war progressed, the Muslim leader abandoned his hope of a peaceful coexistence.

mirthless laugh. He is intolerant, anti-Serb, and authoritarian." Leading up to the war, Tudjman had openly violated the rights of his 12 percent Croatian Serb minority, dismissing them from work, requiring them to take loyalty oaths, and subjecting them to attacks on their homes and property. If there is a driving force behind the current Balkan crisis, it is the extreme enmity that rages between Croat and Serb leadership over these crimes and, more importantly, those of the Second World War.

Serbian president Slobodan Milošević is a man whom many observers agree is ultimately most responsible for the war in Bosnia and its most egregious trampling of human rights. Zimmerman observed:

> Milosovic is an opportunist, not an idealogue, a man driven by power rather than nationalism. He has made a Faustian pact with nationalism as a way to gain and hold personal power. He is a man of extraordinary coldness. I never saw him moved by an individual case of human suffering nor did I ever hear him say a charitable or generous word about any human being, not even a Serb.

Radovan Karadzic, the leader of the Bosnian Serbs, is a big, friendly man with a flamboyant shock of salt-and-pepper hair. A psychiatrist by profession, his leadership of the Bosnian army suggests another, far darker side. Ambassador Zimmerman remarked:

I learned from experience that his outstanding characteristics were his stubbornness and deep-seated hostility to Muslims, Croats, and any other non-Serb ethnic group in his neighborhood. He turned out to be the architect of massacres in the Muslim villages, ethnic cleansings, and artillery attacks on civilian populations.

By the time Richard Holbrooke was shuttling between the various leaders, Karadzic and his chief military commander, General Ratko Mladic, had already been indicted for war crimes by the International War Crimes Tribunal for the former Yugoslavia. Because of that, they were not invited to the summit meetings Holbrooke proposed. It was agreed that Milošević would talk for them though their phantom presence would definitely be felt.

The focus

Whatever peace talks Richard Holbrooke hoped to establish, he knew, would have to be centered on Bosnia. That country still contained the most opposing troops contesting more territory than any other in the Balkans. It had also taken the worst physical beating of the war, destroying its civilian infrastructure, and had seen more human suffering than any of the other newly formed nations, much at the hands of indicted war criminals. And, in the end, a new constitutional government would have to be established partitioning Bosnia-Herzegovina and dispensing power in such a way as to accurately reflect the ethnic composition of its population. All of these problems had to be addressed and solved to the satisfaction of four of the most disagreeable national leaders on the planet.

Any hope of reaching an accord depended first upon changing the battle-drawn boundaries existing within Bosnia in the summer of 1995; boundaries that had been dearly paid for with

Although a psychiatrist by profession, Radovan Karadzic proved to be a ruthless leader of the Bosnian Serbs. Karadzic, who is an indicted war criminal, is believed to have masterminded massacres and ethnic cleansings in which Muslims and Croats were brutally slaughtered.

the sacrifice of men whose deaths the living had sworn to avenge. As the boundaries stood then, they were unacceptable to all concerned, and no one side was willing to give up its hard-won territory to allow it to be redrawn to Holbrooke's specifications. But in the most ghoulish irony of the war, cruel fate raised hopes for a Balkan peace.

Boundaries: Imagined and real

The map and preliminary constitution that Richard Holbrooke and President Clinton's national security advisor, Anthony Lake, had prepared for Bosnia looked good on paper. It gave 49 percent of the Bosnian territory to the Bosnian Serbs—the proposed semiautonomous Serbian Republic within Bosnia—and 51 percent to the Bosnian Croats and Muslims combined—the would-be Federation of Bosnia-Herzegovina. The proposed boundaries would give Karadzic's Serbs a wide, "ethnically pure" swath of eastern and northern Bosnia. Holbrooke wanted the Muslims and Croats to live together in central and western Bosnia, where they would jointly govern their 51 percent. Together, the Serbian Republic and the Muslim-Croat Federation would federally govern the entire nation of Bosnia.

There was a problem, however. The fighting had not separated the warring factions so neatly, and no side was

A tractor becomes a temporary shelter for this man and his family after they used it to escape the war in Bosnia-Herzegovina for the relative safety of Serbia.

"While we have your attention, how about signing a peace treaty?"

about to give up any of their blood-bought territory just to tidy up some foreign diplomat's map. Consequently, while Holbrooke and others dreamed up their scheme, few believed that it had any chance of success. Then came the summer campaign of 1995.

In the wake of the U.S./NATO bombings of the Bosnian Serbs and the U.S.-brokered alliance of Bosnian Muslims and Croats, the Croat-Muslim forces swept the Serbs, soldiers and civilians alike, out of Croatia, northwest and central Bosnia, and from around Sarajevo. The Serbs' own offensive cleared eastern and northern Bosnia of non-Serbs, including ill-fated Srebrenica in the east. The blitz-styled battling continued until, by August 1995, a "miracle" had occurred. The actual fighting had redrawn the boundary lines to match those of Holbrooke's plan, and he seized the opportunity to exploit the fortuitous change.

Throughout September, Richard Holbrooke conducted shuttle meetings all over Europe, the Balkans, and the United States. Pacing, drinking, and smoking hard, he inexhaustibly ramrodded point after snagging point through the diplomatic machinery until enough foundational ground had been laid for President Clinton to announce a cease-fire beginning in October 1995.

"The cease-fire will last sixty days," the president said, "during which time proximity talks will take place, leading eventually to a comprehensive treaty to be signed in Paris." The president chose Wright-Patterson Air Force Base in Dayton, Ohio, as the site of these momentous talks, believing that location would best enhance Bosnia's last hope for peace.

Why Dayton?

Many throughout the international diplomatic community were perplexed as to why Clinton chose a little-known and out-of-the-way place like Dayton, Ohio, as the site of such a potentially historic conference. Paris, London, Moscow, and Washington, D.C., had always been the kinds of cities that hosted them. The president knew, however, that an air force base might best channel the egotistical, posturing, and blustery egos of these Balkan leaders. There, his negotiators could deny them the opportunity to "play to the cameras," set each of them up in identical, humbling accommodations, and keep their face-to-face meetings and hence their showy outrages to a minimum.

These "proximity talks"—so-called because the participants were close to but not present with each other—proved to be highly advantageous for the assistant secretary of state. Using that format, Mr. Holbrooke hopped from Serbia's Milošević to Croatia's Tudjman to

Bosnia's Izetbegović and back again finding out what concessions they were willing to make and what demands they insisted upon. Being separated from each other allowed the former Yugoslav leaders to entertain proposals that might otherwise have caused them to "lose face" if they did so in public. Holbrooke's anticipated application of browbeating, profanity, and sleep deprivation also accelerated the negotiation process.

A hurricane of diplomacy

The conference convened on November 1, 1995, and lasted a whirlwind twenty-one days. Holbrooke blitzed through the first eight days strengthening the ties between the Bosnian Croats and Muslims (the decided underdogs) in order for them to present a unified front against the more dominant Serbs. Also, he wanted to lay the groundwork for the proposed Muslim-Croat Federation that he considered foundational to the agreement.

He hounded the leaders for the next three days, hammering out terms between the Croats and the Serbs over eastern Croatia (Slavonia); they called for the remaining Serbs to relinquish the ground they had won at the beginning of the war and for the separation of belligerents to be monitored by the Russians, traditional allies of the Serbs. Holbrooke powered into the last and most difficult period of negotiations, bending arms to settle the territorial and political issues. Surprisingly, Slobodan Milošević turned out to be the most helpful of the presidents while Izetbegović and Tudjman, due to their victories and momentum at the end of the fighting, proved to be the least willing to bargain.

Nevertheless, the three principal Balkan presidents signed the Peace Agreement on Bosnia and Herzegovina on November 21, 1995, officially ending the three-and-a-half-year Bosnian War. It would remain to be seen whether these Dayton accords would prove practicable when applied, but at least there was a game plan now, with rules whose infractions could be observed. It is perhaps portentous to note, however, that none of the Balkan signatories would look any of the others in the eye at the official

On November 21, 1995, Presidents Slobodan Milošević, Alija Izetbegović, and Franjo Tudjman (seated, from left to right) sign the Dayton peace accords, thus ending the war in Bosnia and creating the foundation for peace in the Balkans.

signing ceremony in Paris. Regardless, they at last had a treaty that covered the five major areas of dispute.

The Dayton accords: A summary

The signatories first agreed to a settlement of the military and security issues fundamental to the success of the Dayton accords. They all realized that if the cease-fire does not hold, then all other attempts to facilitate peace will fail. The treaty members accepted a NATO-led Implementation Force (IFOR) to separate any opposing soldiers who remained intertwined and to establish demilitarized zones of separation between them. They gave the IFOR commander on site the authority to use deadly force to implement the agreement.

Concerning territory, the accords provide for the establishment of a unified state, Bosnia and Herzegovina. It is to be made up of two entities: the Federation of Bosnia and Herzegovina—a blending of Croats and Muslims—and the Republika Srpska, or Bosnian Serbs. In addition, Sarajevo will serve as the national capital, and the Muslims will keep the Serb-surrounded city of Goražde and a land corridor connecting it to the Federation of Bosnia and Herzegovina; and the accords determined that the control of Serb-held Brčko will be arbitrated within one year.

Thirdly, the Dayton accords mandate that Bosnia will implement a new constitution to define and support its double-entity federal system. The constitution prescribes several federal systems. It establishes that the central government in Sarajevo will conduct policies maintaining foreign policy and trade, citizenship and immigration, and monetary issues. The presidency will be shared by three people at a time: a Serb, a Croat, and a Muslim. The chair of the presidency will rotate among the three members. Also, the constitution provides for a central bank, a federal court system, and a bicameral parliament.

The Bosnian War proved to be especially harsh on the civilians and this generated the fourth area of compromise. To help in the survivors' transformation from destruction

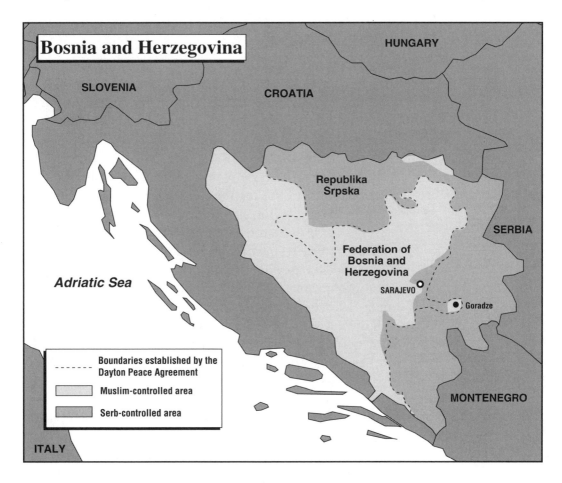

and anarchy to some degree of civil order, the signers of the accords agreed to internationally supervised Bosnian national elections to be held in September 1996. In the process, they accepted the need for a multinational police force and that of international agencies to administer the promised funding for the physical rebuilding of Bosnia.

The final area that the Dayton accords address includes human rights, refugees, and war crimes. Anticipating that the tens of thousands of ethnically cleansed wanderers might be denied the right to cross borders in search of homes, the accords guaranteed their freedom of movement. To politically neutralize accused war criminals, the treaty bans them from public life while demanding that all sides cooperate with the prosecution of war crimes.

A time to praise?

Referring to the finished agreement in Dayton, a British journalist wrote, "It is a triumph for the U.S. government, which, almost single-handedly, took over the task of peacemaking. In the end, the Americans virtually imprisoned the Balkan negotiators for weeks in the depths of Middle America until they signed."

However, another overseas journalist complained, "The agreement was force-delivered by forceps. It is wrought with compulsion rather than compromise and contains many unaddressed flare-up points."

Either way, two undisputable facts stand out regarding the Dayton Peace Agreement. First, the United States were able to broker it when many other nations and international groups had failed in their attempts and, second, it is imperfect. There are reasons to both praise and criticize both the accords and the diplomacy that created them. Perhaps, though, all praise and criticism should be withheld until the treaty's ultimate success or failure can be assessed. After all, there are as many challenges to its implementation as there are steps in the journey to peace, and it is up to the NATO Implementation Force to begin surmounting them.

4

Operation Joint Endeavor: Pulling the Brawlers Apart

THE SNOW WAS already drifting waist-deep and the fog was hanging low when the first American soldiers of the NATO Implementation Force reached Bosnia. They made it just in time to spend Christmas 1995 in wooden-floored tents that kept out the cold reasonably well but offered none of their families' warmth. Outside in the frostbiting temperatures, they performed tasks ranging from setting up radar and satellite communication equipment to bulldozing shell craters in airport runways. Their fingers and toes numbed up and tingled as they worked and their breath seemed to freeze in front of their faces.

No complaints

These men, mostly from the U.S. Army's 1st Armored Division, did not complain, however, at least not while the media listened in. Among themselves, some did grouse about not being able to display the American flag and drink beer, but they performed their high- and low-tech jobs professionally, rapidly, and generally with high morale. There was an unspoken tension, though, suspended in the brooding fog. Unidentified vehicles and people caused sensible alarm. For these one thousand widely deployed men represented a mere advance guard and their small numbers in this wilderness of hatred required that they maintain extreme vigilance.

The forces, the freedoms, and the limitations

The Operation Joint Endeavor force responsible for implementing the military, security, and territorial mandates of the Dayton peace accords would ultimately consist of 60,000 international troops from thirty-two countries, including such diverse nations as Luxembourg, which promised 300 soldiers; Norway, 750; Finland, 750; and Pakistan, 1,000. The largest contingents were to come from Germany, France, the United Kingdom, and the United States, with deployments of 5,000, 13,000, 14,000, and 20,000 men, respectively.

U.S. admiral Leighton W. Smith Jr., overall commander of IFOR, had learned a lesson about how he would command these troops from the UN leaders who had mishandled their Blue Helmets during their three-and-a-half-year deployment in Bosnia. He had watched those dedicated soldiers suffer greatly due to restrictions put on their use of weapons and by a general reluctance on the part of UN diplomats to "antagonize" the warring factions in any way. Hundreds of the UN peacekeepers had been kidnapped, beaten, held hostage, and otherwise abused. Bosnians, who had no reason to fear reprisals, had killed some 156 of them.

Admiral Smith, "Snuffy" to his friends, demanded from the Dayton negotiators that his troops have much more latitude in the use of their weapons and that they be supported by the deployment of tanks, artillery, and airpower. He also insisted that they be allowed to "carry heavy weapons and shoot them not only if they come under fire but even if they are just threatened and to be able to fire them if anyone even points a gun at them in a menacing fashion."

That notwithstanding, Admiral Smith still balanced

U.S. admiral Leighton Smith (right) shakes hands with a French commander after a press conference in Sarajevo. Smith became the overall commander of NATO's Implementation Force (IFOR), whose goal was to ensure the Dayton accords were adhered to by all sides.

his men's right to defend themselves with the admonition that they employ restraint. "We're not cowboys looking for a fight," he said as the mission began. "We've got to keep the warring sides apart. It's the guys coming in here with the checkbooks and the cranes and the bulldozers that will make a difference in this country." However, those checkbooks and cranes and bulldozers would never get the chance to rebuild Bosnia if Admiral Smith and his IFOR troops did not first lay the groundwork.

The military mission

The Dayton signatories mandated that the Implementation Forces enforce several accord articles related to the military aspects of the peace settlement. Within those articles, the following passages are perhaps most relevant to the success of the military mission. The first, the cessation of hostilities, requires that IFOR ramrod "an end to the tragic conflict in the region" and ensure that the parties "refrain from all offensive operations of any type against each other." Second, they are to supervise the "withdrawal of foreign forces" and remove all "individual advisors, freedom fighters, trainers, volunteers, and personnel from neighboring and other states." Third, IFOR must promote the "withdrawal of all Bosnian forces behind a zone of separation which shall be established on either side of the Agreed Ceasefire Line [the Inter-Entity Boundary Line—as it is officially called—keeping the newly formed Serbian Republic and Muslim-Croat Federation apart]."

Secondary tasks include destroying mines, exchanging prisoners, "co-operating with the war crimes tribunal," building bridges and repairing roads necessary for IFOR movements, enforcing "no-fly" zones, clearing roadblocks, isolating Balkan tanks and artillery, and disarming resistant soldiers. It is easy to see how the term "mission creep," the

A Muslim family watches an armed U.S. soldier patrol their neighborhood. While stationed in Bosnia, U.S. peacekeepers were heavily armed and allowed to fire their weapons when threatened or under fire.

A U.S. Marine visits young refugees at a food distribution center in Mogadishu, Somalia. IFOR officials closely studied the mistakes made during the 1992 mission in Somalia to avoid crossing what they termed the "Mogadishu line."

straying from specific objectives, became widely used in the discussion of the IFOR role and how the incident that coined it haunted the NATO commanders so.

A lesson learned

In 1992 U.S. troops went to Somalia in the eastern "horn" of Africa to aid in that starvation-ridden country's "national reconciliation and reconstruction." Their mission was clearly stated as being solely a humanitarian one in spite of the civil war raging in and around the lawless capital of Mogadishu. However, American strategy planners soon decided that it was the bloody competition between private gangsters, or "warlords," that was preventing the feeding of the people so they ordered U.S. troops to expand their mission—allowing it to creep away from its original focus—to include quashing the warring gangs.

The well-armed gangsters did not quash that easily, though. In fact, they proved to be tenacious foes. And when the world watched eighteen U.S. Army Rangers die in a televised firefight, with the taunting gangmen debauched by dragging at least one dead American through the streets, the message became seared into the planners' minds: don't ever cross the "Mogadishu line" again; don't let your mission creep.

Keeping that lesson in mind, General John Shalikashvili, chairman of the U.S. Joint Chiefs of Staff, summed up the IFOR military mission in Bosnia by insisting what it is not. In a December 1995 interview, he said:

> The Implementation Force will not be responsible for the conduct of humanitarian operations. It will not be a police force. It will not conduct nation-building. It will not be a disarmament force and chase after people to collect weapons and whatnot. And it will not be responsible for the movement of refugees.

While changing political winds may force General Shalikashvili to broaden his view of the mission, the sixty thousand IFOR troops in Bosnia have plenty of work to do right now even with his laundry list of exemptions. And it must be done by Christmas of 1996 according to the original timetable. But what has IFOR accomplished thus far and how much do they have left to do? And what has it been like for these individual peacekeepers adrift in Bosnia's cauldron of boiling enmity?

IFOR: The initial phase

During the first weeks following the signing of the Dayton Peace Agreement, the few NATO forces in Bosnia belonged primarily to the French and British contingents. They were the remnants of the UN Blue Helmets who stayed on after the UN pulled out, and it was their experience that made them snicker just a little at the initial ineptitude of the first arriving Americans.

The French and British had already removed two-thirds of the roadblocks in the country, occupied a dam to prevent its being sabotaged, and mapped out hundreds of square miles of minefields. They had started negotiations with the various Bosnian factions for the disengagement of their troops and built bridges and roads to facilitate the refugees' freedom of movement.

The Europeans, however, did not lord their accomplishments over the Americans who were trickling in. One of their officers referred to the U.S. matériel already contributed, conceding, "None of us would be here in green vehicles marked IFOR if it weren't for the Americans. We don't even have to see them for there to be a difference." And it was not long before increasing numbers of Americans began to arrive to undertake responsibilities comparable to those of the French and British.

They occupied the northern sector of Bosnia and set up 1st Armored Division headquarters at Tuzla. C-130 Hercules air transports braved fog, snow, and ice to land troops and supplies. Amazingly, a C-130 landed, unloaded, and took off every twenty minutes. At least one carrying relief supplies took gunfire early on from unidentified snipers. Bullets also zipped by a British helicopter transporting two sick children and their mothers through the British-controlled western sector to Sarajevo. These incidents caused no casualties, but they served as disconcerting warnings nonetheless.

A French soldier surveys the damage caused by a Serbian attack. In Bosnia, UN peacekeepers from France and England initiated the rebuilding of Bosnia's infrastructure and made it possible for refugees to move about the region unimpeded.

The Changing UN Mission:

Along the Croatian border, American combat engineers completed a troublesome float-bridge across the Sava River, and the main force of men, tanks, trucks, and fighting vehicles started rumbling into Bosnia. A reporter pondered the sight and wrote, "The bridge settled six to eight inches under the weight of the tanks and water came up above their tracks. It looked as if the tanks were gliding across the top of the currents." As poetic as that image may have been, those tanks represented all the firepower that would ever be needed to silence the guns of the warring sides, if such force should be required.

Just doing their jobs

Before Christmas, IFOR patrols began confronting Bosnian troops from varying factions. The British demanded possession of a Serbian antiaircraft gun. The gunners grumbled but complied. A Serb got the last word, though, calling ominously after the Brits, "We still have an army and we still know how to fight!"

IFOR soldiers take cover behind a burned truck as they clear mines from the Sarajevo suburb of Stup. Clearing mines continues to be a top priority for the NATO forces.

Land mines became a problem almost immediately, all three million of them. Mine detectors even discovered them within the U.S. Army headquarters encampment at Tuzla along pathways that were being routinely traversed. One of the soldiers ordered to safely detonate them said flatly, "They're Yugoslav mines that wouldn't kill you but would smash your legs, and you'd have four soldiers carrying you away in pain."

The U.S. headquarters personnel were lucky. They miraculously stepped where the mines weren't. Since then, over fifty others have not been so fortunate. More than a dozen among the victims have died from mine explosions so far. When asked if these casualties were giving President Clinton any second thoughts about the mission, he replied confidently, "No, not at all. I told the American people before it all started that the place was filled with mines." And indeed, clearing them is still one of IFOR's most important responsibilities.

IFOR troops have incurred several other deaths and many injuries as a result of them "just doing their jobs." Most of the casualties have resulted from incidents not directly related to combat weaponry, but to those who have suffered them, they are just as grievous as bullet wounds. Trucks have collided and armored personnel carriers have plummeted from cliffs, causing every conceivable broken bone, laceration, or concussion. Fingers have been mashed; toes have been frozen. At least one man has died of a heart attack.

Despite the dangers, the IFOR troops have managed to enforce the separation of warring factions surprisingly well and place them on the appropriate sides of their separation zones. That has entailed jobs as mundane as posting road signs in the correct languages and as dangerous as convincing armed, angry men to go home. Near Sarajevo,

Heavily armed IFOR soldiers patrol an abandoned Bosnian Serb village to make sure that the warring parties have separated in compliance with the Dayton accords.

one Muslim soldier shouted at IFOR troops, "We can't trust NATO to keep the Serbs out! We have to keep our own people here, too!" It took several tense hours to convince the Muslims to leave. In the divided city of Mostar, the Muslims and Croats never did completely abandon their urban positions opposing each other.

Riskier jobs and a few more failures

In other disappointments, Bosnian factional troops have continued to detain one another—sometimes for days—at various checkpoints, and IFOR has not been able to secure the release of them all in a timely fashion. Neither were they able to prevent a hand grenade from killing one and maiming nineteen others who were riding on a Sarajevo streetcar.

French IFOR troops have had to stand by and watch the Serbs of Sarajevo burn their own neighborhoods and flee rather than live under Muslim rule as planned for in the Dayton accords. A Serb leader spoke for most of his people when he cried, "Serbs in Sarajevo will not accept Muslim rule! We will organize ourselves and put up armed resistance to the establishment of a Muslim administration!" The French peacekeepers had to let the house fires burn and settle for guarding water, gas, and electrical stations outside of town.

Strict rules of engagement, designed to prevent mission creep, prevented them from apprehending arsonists unless they were caught in the act of starting the fires. And despite IFOR's insistence that its soldiers may engage belligerents, the underlying tone of the mission has been to avoid confronting them if at all possible.

A firmer stance

When incidents of sniping increased in Sarajevo, however, French antisniper teams were finally allowed to fire back on gunmen in Serbian neighborhoods. Afterward a NATO spokesman announced, "Several shots have been fired at our troops in recent days. In light of the increased danger to our troops, a security operation was launched to put an end to it." And, indeed, it did.

IFOR got tough with another faction when an armed group of Muslims attempted to transport several truckloads of guns, rocket launchers, and mortars across the zone of separation near Mostar and would not respond to Spanish peacekeepers who tried to stop them. The IFOR men called in air support and two U.S. jets circled menacingly until the Muslims turned the arms over. An Implementation Force spokesman explained, "We've found that Thunderbolt airplanes are fairly effective at gaining adherence to the Dayton Accords. Our policy is no weapons in the zone of separation and that is non-negotiable. We find them, we take them, period."

In a scene fit for Clint Eastwood, a U.S. colonel squared off with Serbian soldiers who had denied IFOR entry into an illegal arsenal for over twenty-four hours. The colonel finally cinched his eyes and asserted, "I want you to know that I am going in with or without your permission. I have above me air support. I have helicopters. I have artillery targeted right here where we are standing and I will use them all if I have to. Now stand aside!" And, after a

Spanish peacekeepers cross the makeshift bridge that joins the Muslim and Croat sectors of Mostar. With the help of IFOR's strength and firepower, Spanish troops were able to keep Muslim forces from stockpiling weapons.

A Serbian man drives a horse-drawn cart past bombed-out houses in Serbian-held Kravice. With the implementation of the Dayton peace accords, civilians in war-stricken areas are once again able to move about freely and slowly start to rebuild their lives.

brooding pause, the Serbs did as they were told.

Muslim terrorists

Some of the most dramatic episodes of treaty enforcement have come at the hands of Special Forces troops. In one, French commandos rappelled from a U.S. Green Beret helicopter in the middle of the night and stormed an Iranian training facility for Bosnian Muslim terrorists located in a three-story ski resort. They karate-chopped the sentry in the neck, rendering him unconscious, and captured another ten Muslims inside, three of whom were Iranian. The IFOR commandos confiscated a veritable arsenal of weapons, booby traps, and bombs designed for terrorist attacks and got the Iranians to admit that they were planning to use them against NATO facilities.

A U.S. State Department spokesman said of the Iranian/Bosnian Muslim scheme, "This is a very serious development. We cannot tolerate foreign fighters who are a threat to our soldiers. It is a clear violation of the Dayton Peace Accords that called for their expulsion by January 19, 1996." As many as five thousand Iranian terrorists are thought to remain in Muslim Bosnia, but they are lying far lower as a result of the Special Forces.

The largest scale standoff took place in July between Bosnian Serbs and Americans. When the Serbs illegally removed some of their tanks from a storage area and formed a defensive perimeter around their mountaintop headquarters, the Americans responded with helicopters, airplanes, and several hundred infantrymen.

For a day and night, the two forces glowered at each other, weapons at the ready. An IFOR spokesman said,

"Some junior Bosnian Serb officers overreacted and made some threats aimed at our helicopters and, of course, we don't tolerate that at all." The Serbs finally yielded after being pressured by the president of Serbia proper, Slobo-dan Milošević, but not before stirring up a riot of angry civilians against the U.S. presence.

A job well done?

As the military mission reached its halfway point, the successes that the IFOR troops had amassed appeared considerable. They had enforced the cease-fire, evacuated the zones of separation, and overseen the exchange of thousands of square miles of contestable land. In addition, they had dispatched the Balkan belligerents and their heavy arms to their respective territories while deporting many unauthorized foreign troops from the country. They had freed prisoners, cleared minefields, and opened high-ways and borders to unimpeded travel. Their greatest achievement, though, was that they had stopped the wide-spread killing, at least long enough for the living to bury the dead.

In May 1996 Richard Holbrooke said of the IFOR mission:

> Let's note that the military aspects of Dayton have been im-plemented almost completely with no loss of life to NATO forces from hostile action. The Bosnian Serbs pulled back on schedule. Sarajevo was united under Muslim control. No one, not even the negotiators at Dayton, would have dared predict this five months ago. Still, it is too early for self-congratulations. Other divided lands, Korea and Cyprus, for example, bear witness to temporary cease-fire lines that turn into permanent dividing lines.

Indeed, the "easy part," the military mission, was over. The most difficult assignment, the rebuilding of the civil-ian nation, loomed forbiddingly ahead.

5

"Free and Fair" Elections: The Elusive Key to a New Government

As THE SUMMER of 1996 wound down, Muslims, Croats, and Serbs were still rooting through the debris of high-rises and smoldering houses for firewood, canned food, and any other salvageable items that might have enhanced their chances of survival. One Muslim man, combing the rubbled streets of Sarajevo, found a toy tank and gave it to his little boy as his only birthday present, the irony escaping them both. Those returning to their homes embraced those who had stayed behind and sobs of anguished reunion usually followed. Often where their homes had been only brick shards and broken glass remained. Seldom did they find all the people whom they had left.

But at least the shooting had stopped and most people could venture outside without fear of snipers or incoming mortar shells. In a few places, they could even cross over once-forbidden borders to visit graves of loved ones or surviving friends on the other side. The same nettlesome questions arose, though, among members of every ethnic faction. What would happen in the next few months? Who would rule over them? And would civil order be maintained after the IFOR forces left?

Building blocks

Before real peace can ever come to Bosnia, the people there will need laws and lawmakers, courts and police forces, schools, fair taxes, and a stable military. They will need homes, land, sewage systems and drinking water, roads, banks, public utilities, and a postal system. But most of all, they will need to be joined with their former enemies into one cohesive whole, a whole in which the composite parts can work together for the mutual benefit of all. But who will oversee a political system with so ambitious a scope? The only hope lies in a legitimately elected federal government and the constitution establishing it.

Annex 4 of the Dayton Peace Agreement addresses this need directly, stating that "Bosnia and Herzegovina shall be a democratic state which operates under the rule of law and with free and democratic elections. They shall consist

During the war, tenants of nearby apartment buildings constructed this corridor of wrecked cars to shield them from snipers while traveling to and from their homes.

of the two Entities, the Federation of Bosnia and Herzegovina and the Republika Srpska." Also, the accords call for Bosnia and Herzegovina to have a federal two-chamber parliamentary assembly, a three-member presidency, and a constitutional court.

Several other points of the Dayton Peace Agreement must be satisfied before the constitution can be put into effect. All parties will have to "observe human rights and the protection of refugees and displaced persons." They must also "cooperate in the investigation and prosecution of war crimes." Finally and most fundamentally, they have to "welcome and endorse the elections program for Bosnia and Herzegovina." For without freely and fairly elected leaders that represent the ethno-religious mixture of Bosnia, there is little hope that any of the three factions will remain in the union.

Paving the way for the first elections

The signatories of the Dayton Peace Agreement anticipated the problems that might arise when the Bosnian factions went to the polls to elect the leaders of the new federal Bosnian government. Accordingly, they added "Annex 3: Agreement on Elections" to the final document. It calls for free and fair elections, the right to vote in private, freedom of expression and of the press, and freedom of movement. In another annex, the agreement specifically banned any indicted war criminals from holding or even running for public office in Bosnia.

The accords mandate that an impartial agency, the Organization for Security and Cooperation in Europe (OSCE), supervise the preparation for and conduct of the elections and determine whether these conditions were being met. If they were not, the OSCE had the option of postponing the elections, which were set for September 14, 1996.

Almost immediately the OSCE began reporting violations among the three competing factions. The Serbs, Croats, and Muslims were all limiting freedom of expression in television, radio, and the print media. All three were restricting freedom of movement across interentity boundaries, and the Bosnian Serbs were openly violating the ban on indicted war criminals holding or running for public office, most flagrantly in the person of President Radovan Karadzic.

As early as April 1996, an OSCE official withdrew his approval of the scheduled election. He stated that he "had assumed that the Serbian separatist leaders who have been indicted for war crimes would have been forced from power by now, that refugees would have the ability to return to their homes, and that all sides would cooperate with international supervisors, none of which has occurred." And matters would get worse before they got better.

A disagreement over timetables

The OSCE's adamant stance frustrated the American/European diplomatic team and President Bill Clinton especially, all of whom had made it clear from the beginning that they wanted to meet the September 14 deadline no matter what. The force with which the Clinton administration pushed to keep the elections on the original schedule prompted a general opinion among world observers that the president was more interested in having the Dayton mandates fulfilled before the U.S. presidential elections in November 1996 than in having the more lasting peace that might have resulted from a postponement of the elections until requisite voting conditions had been met. Political critics were quick to note that events in Bosnia even resembling a Clinton diplomatic success would have aided his chances of reelection whether those events ultimately brought peace to the Balkans or not.

There were other arguments that U.S. and European officials cited to justify pursuing a rapid, if imperfect, consummation of the Bosnian elections. A former U.S. ambassador said:

> Keeping the elections on schedule is a way to keep pressure on the parties because that drives the parties to do what they need to do with respect to refugees, return of refugees, free movement of people, access to media, everything we need

President Clinton reviews troops at the U.S. military headquarters in Tuzla. Some critics have argued that Clinton's efforts to keep the Bosnian elections on schedule were motivated more by his desire for reelection than the establishment of a lasting peace in the Balkans.

for democratic elections. I don't want to lose momentum and I think the elections are critical to that momentum.

Western officials never claimed that ideal circumstances existed for "free and fair" elections. However, many did see prompt elections as a possible chance for establishing federal institutions that could eventually create those circumstances. And while those institutions would undoubtedly be weak and problematic at first, they would at least be in existence and have a fighting chance to survive. Postponing the elections, they believed, would have been tantamount to eliminating them altogether.

One European diplomat put it this way:

It is a terrible dilemma for us. We all know the situation is bad. People who try to cross from one side to the other get beaten and harassed and eventually go back. But if we don't certify the elections, the ethnic partitions will remain and ethnic cleansing will be rewarded. Elections and the attempt to establish federal institutions are all we have left.

A U.S. envoy added pragmatically, "The Dayton agreement does not say that we have to have a perfectly functioning democracy in place in order to hold the elections. In fact, the elections are there to lay the framework for a functioning democracy."

Reasons to wait

Groups who favored postponing the vote made claims that sounded just as reasonable as those made by the elections-at-any-cost contingent. Human Rights Watch/Helsinki issued a statement warning:

> Unless immediate and decisive steps are taken to enforce respect for human rights, ensure the right to return for refugees and displaced persons, and bring to justice those responsible for war crimes, the elections which the U.S. Secretary of State insists should go forward in September will be a charade. While holding the elections in Bosnia may be in the best interest of Mr. Clinton's reelection campaign, it is certainly not in the best interest of a Bosnia that is not partitioned along ethnic lines, and where the ethnic slaughter of thousands is not simply forgotten in an effort by foreign governments not to upset their own domestic political agendas.

Indeed, without freedom of movement, potential voters would have been unable to return to their original residences to participate in the elections. And many cases had already been reported of the various factions denying the reentry of opposing ethnic group members to keep their votes from "spoiling" election results.

And there was the problem of the media. Unless it was free, voters could only get to hear the one-sided opinions of the faction that happened to control the newspapers, radio, and television stations. And since ultranationalists who wanted to separate from the new Bosnia controlled that media, "news" had become propaganda and voters were having to decide issues based upon inflamed rhetoric instead of balanced information.

As far as indicted war criminals were concerned, if they were not apprehended or otherwise neutralized, they would have participated in the political process either directly or indirectly. That would have implicitly condoned their criminal acts, undermining the authority of the entire Dayton peace process and reinforcing the ethnic separatist ideology that they so prejudicially espoused.

A Bosnian diplomat summed up the reasons to postpone the September 14 elections by saying that if they were held as scheduled, they "would only help Karadzic's hardliners win international legitimacy. Once they win international auspices they can really crack down on democracy, on refugees, seal their borders, do whatever they want." The diplomat went on to predict that the Bosnian Serb Republic would then attempt to secede from the new federal Bosnia and join Greater Serbia, breaking Bosnia into warring factions once again.

And what about Karadzic?

Radovan Karadzic is perhaps the most beloved political leader in the Balkans today, at least among his own people. He and every other ethnic leader are despised by all former enemy factions. That is to be expected. But no other Balkan politician, including Milošević, Izetbegović, and Tudjman, comes close to garnering the admiration, respect, and hero-worship that this poet/psychiatrist does at home. While the reasons for that adoration may not be altogether clear to outsiders, his combination of intelligence, charisma, and dedication to his people certainly contribute. Whatever the reasons though, the great majority living in Republika Srpska always opposed his stepping down, especially if it was to be in response to foreign pressures.

That, however, had been exactly what the "foreigners" had been demanding ever since the War Crimes Tribunal in The Hague, Holland, in-

Although the war crimes tribunal had charged him with committing genocide, and Muslim and Croat leaders demanded his resignation from power, Radovan Karadzic remained a hero to the Bosnian Serbs.

dicted Karadzic for "genocide, rape, murder, and crimes against humanity" for the killing or removal of Bosnian Muslims and Croats during ethnic cleansings. The tribunal did not claim to have evidence that Karadzic personally took part in any of the alleged atrocities but rather that he planned and ordered them.

The Dayton peace talks, which Karadzic as an indicted war criminal had not been allowed to attend, determined that "no person convicted or indicted of war crimes shall hold or run for political office in Bosnia." Not surprisingly, Radovan Karadzic's refusal to leave office had become a major impediment to the election process; so much so that the Muslim and Croat leaders said they would boycott the September 14 elections as long as he remained in power.

In May 1996 Carl Bildt, the Swedish diplomat responsible for the civilian aspects of the Bosnian peace, said, "Dr. Karadzic is actively disrupting the peace process. By his activities, he is poisoning the political atmosphere and accordingly threatening the very political process that is going to lead us up to elections."

For his part, Karadzic simply offered, "No one can arrest me, because that would provoke the death of many soldiers from the western alliance, and my people will defend me. No one can act like a boss in my country." And, indeed, it appeared for some time that he might be right.

The limits of "cooperation"

With sixty thousand heavily armed troops in Bosnia ready to pounce at a moment's notice, it did not seem unreasonable to ask them to capture just one man, even if that man was Radovan Karadzic. That was certainly how the War Crimes Tribunal in The Hague and human rights activists all over the world viewed it anyway. But when Admiral Leighton Smith, the top IFOR commander at the time, was asked if he would order such a capture, he replied cheerily, "Absolutely not. I don't have any authority to arrest anybody." And strictly interpreting the Dayton accords, he did not.

Operating strictly under the Dayton Peace Agreement, IFOR troops did not have the authority to actively pursue and arrest indicted war criminals. However, soldiers could detain suspects if they encountered them during routine patrols.

Operating under the Dayton mandate that required only "cooperating with" the War Crimes Tribunal, IFOR wanted to avoid any mission creep that might carry them over the "Mogadishu line," and they limited themselves to a policy of arresting indicted war criminals only if they "bumped into them." And Dr. Karadzic had always been far too shrewd to let that happen. Besides, he had already been identified several times well within reach of IFOR troops and had not been confronted.

A U.S. State Department spokesman tried to justify that, saying:

> There is still pretty much of an agreement that IFOR soldiers won't go into the hills hunting for war criminals. There are a lot of young platoon commanders, second lieutenants, just waiting for the opportunity [for Karadzic to bump into them]. That's what medals are made of.

As of July 1996, however, neither Karadzic nor a medal had been forthcoming. Clearly, another approach would have to be tried and this time it would be political.

Stepping down or just moving over?

Western diplomats eager for Karadzic's removal had not been lying idle waiting for the IFOR troops to do the job. They had been applying pressure to Serbian president Slobodan Milošević, the patron of Karadzic's Bosnian Serbs. At the signing of the Dayton Peace Agreement, Richard Holbrooke had insisted that Milošević agree to push the Bosnian Serb leader out of power. Milošević had agreed but then proceeded to do absolutely nothing.

Carl Bildt, representing the Europeans, stepped up the coercion by threatening to renew the damaging economic and financial sanctions on Rump Yugoslavia that had only recently been lifted after eighteen devastating months. He said, "Milosovic has signed the peace agreement and he has a very distinct responsibility for the implementation of every part of it. There are no exceptions."

John Kornblum, the chief U.S. Bosnia coordinator, underscored the effort, announcing, "You can say I have stated [to Milošević] that the United States and the Contact Group [the United States, Britain, France, Germany, and Russia] would definitely move to reimpose economic and trade sanctions on Rump Yugoslavia if Karadzic does not step down."

Milošević, whose Yugoslav Serbs had amply supported the Serbs in Bosnia, finally took the message to heart and threatened sanctions of his own against Karadzic, forcing the good doctor to give up the nominal leadership of the Bosnian Serb Republic. But he did so at a cost. Many Bosnian Serbs began considering Milošević, their one-time hero, to be a traitor. Karadzic himself said as much even though the Milošević-brokered agreement appears to have allowed Karadzic to stay in power behind the scenes.

Richard Holbrooke, only partially satisfied with the deal, remarked, "This is a minimally acceptable package." However, Karadzic's moving over, if not out, seemed to appease those in favor of election postponement enough for them to support the September vote date.

A test case

The September national elections were not the first ones held in Bosnia in 1996. The partitioned city of Mostar in southern Herzegovina had theirs in June. The supposed alliance between Croats and Muslims so critical to the success or failure of the Dayton accords came under intense scrutiny during citywide polling there, and the results did not inspire confidence in the subsequent Bosnian elections.

The Muslims inhabiting the east side of Mostar's dividing river had threatened to boycott the elections for city council, claiming that seventy thousand of the original Muslim population would be unable to vote because they had been driven out to foreign countries. The Muslim mayor said, "The elections cannot go ahead until all the

Citizens of Mostar stroll along the eastern embankment of the Neretva River. Muslims living in the eastern part of Mostar threatened to boycott the elections held there in June 1996 because a large portion of the original population had been relocated during the war and would be unable to vote.

people who were in Mostar in 1991 can vote. Otherwise, what we would be doing is legalising ethnic cleansing and ethnic genocide and we will not allow that."

After considerable civic unrest—a few murders, many beatings, and destruction of churches and mosques—the Croats agreed to allow Bosnian Muslims abroad to vote by absentee ballot. Although, according to a Croat spokesman, "it was clear in the negotiations in Dayton that the refugees absent from Mostar would not be entitled to vote, just as those displaced people now living in Mostar who were not registered to vote in 1991 are excluded."

Regardless, the Mostar election was held on June 30, 1996, albeit with many hitches, including a one-month postponement that the Muslims had demanded. While the Muslims were happy enough with their winning majority, the loss drove the Croats deeper into the confines of their own side of town, complaining that the vote tally had been manipulated and that they would not take part in the joint government until a court ruled on the validity of the elections. Croatian president Tudjman, pressured by American diplomats, passed the pressure on to the Bosnian Croats to have them delay any separatist action until after the September national elections, making September 14 an even more anticipated date.

The big show

For all its apprehension, however, September 14 came and went with generally less violence and agitation than anyone thought possible. Some observers even sensed a letdown of sorts. There were fistfights, to be sure, and border obstructions, and rocks thrown at buses, but no one died and few were injured. All in all, the day passed without serious incident. Under the watchful eye of IFOR forces, the tally went as expected: Muslims voted for Muslims, Serbs voted for Serbs, and Croats cast their ballots for Croats. Muslim Alija Izetbegović, Serb Momcilo Krajisnik, and Croat Kresimir Zubak won slots on the three-man presidency with Izetbegović serving as first chairman since he garnered more votes than the other two.

Muslim refugees line up to vote during the September 14, 1996, elections in Doboj, Bosnia, the first elections held after nearly three and a half years of war.

It is too early to determine how much the elections really cemented the chances for a Bosnian government and federation. Indeed, in the wake of the polling results, each side threatened to nullify the tally due to the other sides' election fraud. Perhaps the manner in which war criminals are eventually dealt will best portend the fate of Bosnia. For if the hatreds caused by the war's atrocities cannot be soothed enough to permit the bloody hands of Bosnia to shake, no amount of voting will allow them to jointly clasp the tools required for reconstruction.

6

Justice or Peace: The War Crimes Tribunal vs. "Realpolitik"

THE BOSNIAN WAR has come to be known more for its massacres than its battles. Few stories have emerged of individual heroism in combat or valor in the face of an equally armed enemy. There have been no medals or tombs for unknown soldiers. No monuments to glory have been consecrated. The only "virtue" to have arisen during these three and a half years of viciousness is so instinctive as to nearly strip it of any honor. That instinct is for survival and it was elicited with painful regularity in Bosnia.

Plenty of need for the stuff

The survival instinct surfaced within the Serbian-run camp near Banja Luka among the Croats who escaped the mass throat-cuttings there and at a similar camp near Prijedor, where Muslims saved themselves from being crushed in the thirst-driven riots that trampled so many others. The will to survive spared hundreds of Croats and Muslims in Brčko when the Serbs murdered hundreds of others after their takeover there early in the war. And while that animalistic ethic did not glorify man, it at least did preserve the many Muslim men whom the Serbs had ordered to kill their fellow prisoners or be killed themselves.

The same survival instinct prevailed when Serbian women hid under the bodies of a hundred other Serb

Prisoners of war eat their daily meal of soup and bread inside a Croatian-run camp. After the war's end, tribunals were established to bring war criminals to justice and punish them for the atrocities they committed during the war.

civilians who had been gunned down in a bus convoy by Croatian paramilitaries near Goražde and when the Serbian Orthodox priests in Vlasenica struggled for life after Muslim soldiers cut off their "blessing" fingers, gouged out their eyes, and mutilated their genitals. That will to live saved elderly Serbian farmers whom the Muslims imprisoned for three weeks and beat repeatedly with steel rods and also delivered the Serbian prisoners of war who pulled through after Muslim soldiers cut off their toes one by one.

Cruelty and its victims predominated the killing fields of Bosnia. Heartless leaders led zealous troops, who turned their wicked passions on civilians. Aware of the mounting crimes these men of all sides were committing, the UN Security Council established the International War Crimes Tribunal for the former Yugoslavia in May 1993, and two years later, the signers of the Dayton peace accords agreed to cooperate with that tribunal.

Why trials?

One of the judges presiding over the Nuremberg trials for Nazi war criminals after World War II said, "The wrongs which we seek to condemn and punish have been so calculated, so malignant, and so devastating that civilization cannot tolerate their being ignored because it cannot survive their being repeated." And while there are not many who believe a repeat of atrocities in Bosnia would doom all the world's civilization, everyone agrees that it would surely consume the remaining Balkan Slavs.

To them, the Bosnian war crimes trials are certainly as justified and necessary as those in Nuremberg, Germany, fifty years ago. They believe that the perpetrators must be punished to quench each aggrieved individual's sense of revenge and to deter the commission of future war crimes. War crimes tribunals, they also know, tend to relieve the collective guilt of those groups whose members committed them. By sacrificing the offending individuals among them on the altar of international justice, the innocent majority are not condemned alike.

According to everyone involved, war tribunal justice is a requirement if the massive transfer of refugees required for the establishment of Bosnia's two new republics is to take effect. "How can I ever go home," one refugee said, "if the man who killed my father goes free?" A war crimes investigator remarked, "The only way anyone will ever feel safe is if those who are responsible for the killings are punished. People explain this war as revenge for the atrocities in the past that were never punished. We have got to stop that cycle."

Prelude to punishment: The indictments

The War Crimes Tribunal has been able to formally indict only fifty-seven suspects: forty-six Serbs, eight Bosnian Croats, and three Bosnian Muslims. The Serbs cite the heavy concentration of Serbian suspects as proof that the tribunal is biased against them. Croats and Muslims counter that more Serbs have been indicted because more Serbs committed crimes. Prosecutors in The Hague have promised to investigate the claims of all factions more vigorously with an eye toward adjusting the balance. The evidence alone of 1995's ethnic cleansings against the

Serbs (primarily by the Croats and Muslims) would warrant broadening the investigations.

The suspects thus far range in rank from commanders of entire detention camps to shift commanders to guards and even visitors. Some were local residents, others were political leaders, and there are a few top military officers. There are those who insist that they were "only following orders." Others say they just watched. Some allegedly planned and carried out the atrocities. The leaders claim that subordinates misread their "intentions."

The allegations include attacking villages, raping women, beating prisoners with metal batons and cables, discharging fire extinguishers into the mouths of prisoners, kicking them with military boots until they died, and hammering nails through their skulls and into their brains. Some suspects allegedly electrocuted their victims, others slit throats, and one colonel is charged with removing 261 men from their hospital beds and having them shot in a field.

A suspected war criminal is photographed after being detained in a Sarajevo jail. Behind him, posters distributed by the Bosnian government identify two Serbian leaders as war criminals.

The prosecutors have diligently prepared strong cases against the initial fifty-seven defendants. The witnesses and the documentation are in order and the wheels of justice are rolling at last. The first four suspects, two Serbs and two Croats, have been processed or are now in custody. For victims demanding satisfaction, however, that is not enough. Many more need to stand trial and the tribunal cannot even apprehend the other fifty-four who are indicted, leaving the prosecutors with the recurring question: Where is the promised cooperation?

In June Human Rights Watch added its voice to the cry by accusing IFOR commander Admiral Leighton Smith of failing to arrest indicted war criminals. Smith fired back his usual response, "IFOR is not authorized to arrest indicted war criminals, nor am I required to attempt to develop intelligence on their whereabouts. We will detain them when and if we come in contact with them during the course of our normal duties." The specters of Mogadishu and mission creep obviously still linger and terrify.

An IFOR soldier looks at wanted posters showing pictures and names of alleged war criminals. Although nearly sixty people have been indicted for war crimes, only a few of the defendants have been apprehended and tried.

According to Article IX of the Dayton accords, "All parties shall cooperate in the investigation and prosecution of war crimes and other violations of international humanitarian law." What that means, in theory, is simple: Serbians are to turn over indicted Serbians, Croats are to turn over indicted Croats, and Muslims are to turn over indicted Muslims. What that all means in practice is equally simple: Serbians resist turning in indicted Serbians, Croats resist turning in indicted Croats, and Muslims resist turning in indicted Muslims (though they have turned over two). However, all three factions seem happy to arrest members of other factions, sometimes when they have not even been formally indicted.

Justice and "Realpolitik" begin to collide

In February 1996 the Bosnian Muslims captured two high-ranking Bosnian Serb officers who had made a wrong turn into Muslim territory near Sarajevo. The Muslims claimed that they had "evidence that both officers participated in killing civilians and also helped organize the killing of civilians." But the officers had not been indicted by the War Crimes Tribunal.

The Serbs angrily protested that their men were "taken to jail without any explanation. They were unarmed and unindicted. The Muslims are making a grave, grave mistake. If these men are not freed, the Muslims will once again find themselves trapped in Sarajevo."

That threat of renewed warfare did not go unheeded. The Dayton diplomats and tribunal investigators rushed to balance the need for peace with that of justice—practical politics, or Realpolitik, versus idealism. In the resulting compromise, they arranged for the release of six other similarly jailed Serbs and formally indicted the two higher officers after which IFOR whisked them off to The Hague. They had, in effect, "bumped into" these two.

This particular crisis came and at least partially went, although it entrenched the Serbs even more deeply in their resistance to the tribunal. No other Balkan governments have cooperated much with the tribunal since that altercation and no more indictments have been handed down. Aside from the occasional threat of economic sanctions, the Western powers have done little to force them to comply with tribunal requests and, as a result, the tenuous peace has held. Temporarily, at least, the sabers have stopped rattling, allowing the practicalities of Realpolitik to prevail over the righteous cry for justice.

The two biggest fish in the indictment sea

Until July 1996 Radovan Karadzic served as the president of the Serbian Democratic Party of Bosnia-Herzegovina, which, in effect, made him the acting (though never elected) president of the self-styled Bosnian Serb Republic. During his term of office, he was twice indicted by the War Crimes Tribunal. The first indictment came in July 1995 for allegedly ordering and maintaining the siege of Sarajevo and for using UN Blue Helmets as hostages. He received the second in November 1995 for allegedly ordering the killing of some six thousand Muslim civilians at Srebrenica. General Ratko Mladic, commander of the Bosnian Serb army, has been similarly charged and is particularly wanted in The Hague for the extreme cruelties he carried out at Srebrenica.

The war crimes tribunal has indicted General Ratko Mladic (left), commander of the Bosnian Serb army, for his part in the gruesome massacre of Muslims at Srebrenica.

Tribunal documents report:

> After Srebrenica fell, a truly terrible massacre of the Muslim population appears to have taken place. The evidence describes scenes of unimaginable savagery: thousands of men executed and buried in mass graves, hundreds of men buried alive, men and women mutilated and slaughtered, children killed before their mothers' eyes, a grandfather forced to eat the liver of his own grandson.

The importance of trying Karadzic and Mladic cries out from Muslim rooftops. If these men are guilty and if they receive a just punishment, then Bosnian Muslims and Croatians might be able to lay down their weapons of revenge. Undoubtedly, IFOR, NATO, the United Nations, and the entire international community consider the two Serb leaders' apprehension to be of the highest importance. So once again the question resounds: Why haven't they handed Karadzic and Mladic over to the War Crimes Tribunal?

The answer, of course, remains the same. IFOR does not want to go over the "Mogadishu line" and let their mission creep into a series of bloody battles with the hardcore Bosnian Serb troops who are defending their beloved leaders. Neither do the Dayton diplomats want to alienate the Bosnian Serbs into pulling out of the newly forming, double-entitied nation of Bosnia, which is the very cornerstone of the Dayton Peace Agreement. And further, it is supposed to be up to the various Balkan factions to police themselves and turn over their own indicted people. Regarding the latter, Richard Holbrooke has said, "It's up to these people. If they don't want peace, they won't have it." And few leaders in Bosnia seem to want it badly enough to turn over their people to foreigners.

The unindictable three

Slobodan Milošević, the Serbian president of Rump Yugoslavia and patron of the Bosnian Serbs, reportedly committed or omitted orders that led to Bosnian Serb atrocities. Franjo Tudjman, president of Croatia and patron of the Bosnian Croats, allegedly ordered or prevented others from stopping acts of Bosnian Croat violence. Alija

Izetbegović, leader of all Bosnia's Muslims, is suspected of encouraging and condoning war crimes committed by his people throughout Bosnia.

"There were only three men in charge of the whole thing," a U.S. official said regarding the war crimes. From them, their offending ethnic protégés in Bosnia "received weapons, uniforms, buses, barracks in which to train 'volunteers,' and everything else they needed to sustain their criminal activities."

Milošević's avowed goal early in the war was the establishment of a Greater Serbia including territory in Bosnia and Croatia, and he vigorously supported the Bosnian and Croatian Serbs who ethnically cleansed Croats and Muslims living there. Tudjman similarly wanted to unite all Balkan Croatians into a "Greater Croatia" under his rule and, toward that end, he quickly came to the aid of the Bosnian Croats in their cleansings of Serbs and Muslims. Izetbegović appears to have gotten a late start on the

Serbian soldiers display their weapons while posing for this January 1994 photograph. During the Bosnian war, the leaders of the warring factions enthusiastically supported the efforts of extremist soldiers like these who participated in ethnic cleansings.

elimination of Serbs and Croats, but that was due to his initial inability to recapture the territory he had lost to them rather than any inherent personal goodness. Troops under his command ultimately committed an increasing number of atrocities as they gained strength during the last year of the war.

Time magazine used Serbian president Milošević as an example of patron leadership, describing how he maintained

> a chain of command linking the JNA [Yugoslav National Army], the Territorial Defense Force [Bosnian Serb army], and the paramilitaries [irregular Serbs] to himself at the top. Using a modern war-fighting principle known as "commander's intent," Milosovic could issue broad orders and leave the details to his subordinates. He could then deny knowledge of his soldiers' acts, no matter how heinous.

Relying upon that thin veneer of "plausible deniability," all three principal leaders in the Bosnian War have been able to avoid any serious threat of indictment by the War Crimes Tribunal. However, that is not the principal reason that these men have enjoyed such unprecedented freedom from prosecution. The Realpolitik, the pragmatic considerations, are far more significant.

Cooperation and rebuilding

Without the continued cooperation of the Dayton Peace Agreement's three primary signatories and their influence over their protégé Serbs, Croats, and Muslims in Bosnia, any hope of rebuilding Bosnia would evaporate into yet another fog of misery. When the Western powers wanted Bosnian Serb president Karadzic to step down, they relied upon Milošević to convince the Bosnian Serb to comply. They counted on Tudjman to strong-arm the Bosnian Croats into at least postponing secession from a Croat-Muslim city government in Mostar and depended upon Izetbegović to convince most of the Iranian terrorists illegally in his country to go back home.

Milošević, Tudjman, and Izetbegović have done all this and more to keep their Bosnian protégés in compliance

"Don't worry, fellas - it'll take them y e a r s to find us!"

with the Dayton accords, in spite of sometimes being called traitors by the most militant among them. However, they have made their diplomatic contributions far more from a desire to avoid economic sanctions than from any honorable quest for peace.

Ironically, these murderous puppeteers will probably escape judgment by the War Crimes Tribunal because they have the greatest chance of ending the killing that they themselves began. In such a case, this would leave Realpolitik as the ultimate victor in Bosnia and the Dayton accords as its primary benefactor. Righteous justice, it seems, would be the tragic loser.

7

Struggling Out of the Ashes: Problems, Solutions, and Still More Problems

FREE AND FAIR elections are critical to the rebuilding of Bosnia. War crimes trials are a must. And compliance with the Dayton accords offers the only real chance of peace, however fragile. But these are just a few of the wide-ranging imperatives brought on in the aftermath of the Bosnian debacle. So many more remain to be addressed.

Roads, bridges, homes, and factories lay in dusty rubble. Electricity, drinking water, gasoline, and food are all in dangerously short supply. The few doctors need medicine for the surfeit of patients, and war-maimed victims need artificial arms and legs. Schools need teachers. Libraries must have books. Without loans, entrepreneurs cannot start the businesses necessary to employ the two million out-of-work Bosnians. And the Muslims, Croats, and Serbs who are supposed to be building a nation together cannot even agree on a common currency.

Financing Bosnia's economic rebuilding will require massive amounts of money, an estimated $5.1 billion over the next four years alone. Consequently, international banks and world organizations representing donor nations such as the United States are beginning to provide it. The

A Croatian family despairingly inspects the ruins of their home. Throughout the former Yugoslavia, people in the process of rebuilding their homes and lives face economic hardships and supply shortages.

one decided advantage to that monetary obligation is that it gives the contributors considerable influence in how those moneys will be spent and President Bill Clinton has applied that leverage fully.

Adding fuel to the firepower

President Clinton has long believed that in order to establish a balance of power in Bosnia, the international community should build up the military of the Muslim-Croat Federation to such an extent that it can defend itself against the superior forces of the Bosnian Serbs. During the war, Clinton encountered rigid opposition to this approach from the Europeans, who feared that more arms would only exacerbate the overall crisis, but Muslim president Izetbegović insisted upon the military aid as a condition for his signing the Dayton Peace Agreement and Clinton's policy won out.

However, as with most things in the Balkans, every silver lining has a cloud and the cloud, in this case, is financial. The United States has ended up having to pay half of the initial $200 million armament bill—with another $600 million to supposedly follow—while the rest of the world nations combined came up with the rest. And the international Muslims have complicated matters further by adding strings to their money. They have demanded that the Croatians within the federation receive none of it because they are not members of the Islamic faith. Similarly, Turkey has already begun training Bosnian Muslim soldiers without including the Croat "infidels." Understandably, this has created even more tension between the Bosnian Muslims and Croats in their already-tense union.

Friends in sly places

Worsening matters (from the Western point of view), Iran is beginning to establish a foothold in Bosnia and, hence, all of Europe. They are "calling in the debts" that the Bosnian Muslims ran up during the war while accepting Iranian arms, supplies, and training by deploying their terrorists there. There are as many as three thousand Iranian Republican Guards—fundamental Islamic holy warriors—reported to be in Bosnia now, many of them legally. "There are loopholes in which the Iranians can hide," a U.S. official said. "They can get married or get Bosnian citizenship. That's their ace in the hole." They not only train the Bosnian Muslims in the techniques of terrorism but they indoctrinate them with their radical Islamic extremism as well.

While President Clinton tacitly approved of the Iranians' presence in Bosnia at the height of the fighting, he now must consider the threat that these avowed terrorists pose to NATO soldiers and to the stability of the peace process in general. The fanatically anti-Western Iranians are said to be goading Bosnian Muslims into resisting the Dayton accords and pushing for a resumption of the war.

Money makes the world go 'round

Ideally, the best hope of preventing hostilities from starting up again is to improve the economy enough so that the three Bosnian communities can clearly see how much they would lose by resuming the fight. The basic needs of shelter, food, health, and livelihood must be provided as "charity" relief initially while economic opportunities are being developed that will enable the Bosnians to eventually earn a living for themselves. This will be expensive.

The UN World Bank has already begun reconstruction projects that will require $1.8 billion in the first year alone. To facilitate farming in the fields and transporting commercial goods on roads, three million land mines are to be cleared. Since the war damaged half of the houses in Bosnia and completely destroyed one-fifth of them, the World Bank intends to repair or replace twenty thousand units in 1996. Also, massive funds will be directed toward restoring the 70 percent of electricity lost due to damaged or gutted power plants. Unemployment will hopefully be ameliorated by insuring that returning soldiers and civilians shelled out of work will get the jobs that these projects generate.

Other necessities to be provided include factory equipment, road-repair machinery, locomotives and railroad-building supplies, buses, and water, sewage, and solid-waste disposal systems. To reestablish communication links between the Bosnians themselves as well as with the rest of the world, phone lines, satellite dishes,

European volunteers assist Croatians in their efforts to rebuild their communities. The UN-operated World Bank has also come to the aid of the Balkans, allotting enormous sums of money for the rebuilding of the infrastructure and economy.

computers, and radio, television, and print news facilities will also be put back on-line.

While reconstructing the physical infrastructure of Bosnia is the primary prerequisite for the rebirth of the economy, longer range needs are not being neglected. The World Bank is rebuilding schools, printing textbooks, and providing classes with educational materials and equipment. They are also repairing farms and introducing modern methods of agriculture. Regarding health, the World Bank is strengthening public health programs, providing drugs and medical equipment, and creating mental and physical rehabilitation programs for war victims.

"We will soon enter a transition from relief to reconstruction," John Menzies, the U.S. ambassador to Bosnia said confidently in May 1996. An American general lyrically noted the "beautiful sounds—the sounds of hammering in the background." Mickey Cantor, the American secretary of commerce sounded a bit less enthusiastic when he said, "We do see opportunities, but they are long term, let's be honest."

In addition to the large-scale destruction of homes in Bosnia, important institutions like schools and hospitals were obliterated by the war. The walls and windows of this elementary school classroom show the severe damage caused by artillery fire.

Speaking of honesty

Even though more money is beginning to come into Bosnia from private industry and relief agencies, the target goal of $5.1 billion over four years is far from being met. It is now likely that the aid will total only $2 billion, and this at a time when the Bosnian ambassador to the United States is estimating that $15 billion will be required. And the amount of money itself is not the only problem.

The bulk of the reconstruction funds are to be funneled through the Bosnian Central Bank, which President Izetbegović's Muslim SDA party controls. Because corruption is so entrenched in Balkan politics, even the most hopeful within the international aid community expect fortunes to be illegally siphoned off by powerful Muslim politicians. "It's going to mean a lot of new Mercedeses for SDA guys around here," one aid administrator said.

And while the majority of the millions will eventually trickle down to the Bosnian Muslims for whom it was intended, much less is expected to reach the Bosnian Serbs, whose lives and property were equally damaged by the war. The reason is simple. The Muslims have local control of most of the money and they resist sharing it with their former enemies. Also, the international powers behind the Dayton accords promised to withhold aid from the Serbs until they turn over their indicted leaders, Radovan Karadzic and Ratko Mladic, to the War Crimes Tribunal for trial. Some aid groups are willing to forego this restriction on the Bosnian Serbs, however, due to the fear that continued exclusion will only drive them more in the direction of war. "We need to do more in Republika Srpska," said a U.S. defense official. "If one of the largest threats to peace is Bosnian Serb soldiers, we need to give them less of a reason to pick their guns back up."

Bosnian Croat gangsterism compounds the aid-distribution problem even further. In Mostar, a Balkan "mafia" has long plied its corrupt trade and, now, wherever reconstruction money appears, it soon attaches its leech lips. One foreign correspondent wrote:

> I have never seen so many European luxury sedans in one place. The Mafia in Mostar and Herzegovina in general are making a killing off of this war—literally. In Muslim Bosnia, a man with a horse and wagon is considered lucky. In Herzegovina, a man isn't a man unless he's driving a Mercedes sport coupe. Such are the disparities.

And disparities are what have always fueled conflict in Bosnia.

A shaky bond

No disparities loom more ominously over the hopes for a Balkan peace than those sundering the Bosnian Croats and Muslims. If the Dayton peace is to take root and grow on its own, the Muslim-Croat Federation must survive. Only together can the two communities neutralize the power of the Bosnian Serbs, but whether they will choose to do so or not remains an open question.

The Bosnian Croats and Muslims began the war allied against the Serbs and fought alongside each other through 1992, but, as often happens in the Balkans, familiarity soon bred contempt and they turned their guns on each other for the next two years. After some of the most gruesome combat of the war, the Americans and Europeans reimposed the original alliance upon the one-time comrades and, again, they went after the Bosnian Serbs. United, they wrested peace from the Serbs at Dayton but, in the absence of a common enemy, they went back to bickering among themselves.

The city of Mostar became the focus of their animosities. It was supposed to have been ethnically remixed and jointly ruled after the war. But, instead, it has split into Croat and Muslim sectors and there has been trouble between them ever since. In January 1996 alone, a Muslim and Croat were killed, two other Muslims were wounded in separate shooting attacks, and several bombs and rockets destroyed shops and homes.

The continuing violence between these supposed allies frustrated one Dayton implementation official enough to threaten, "If I get the impression that the Croats and Muslims do not want a federation and a united Mostar, then we have nothing to do here." And Mostar represents only the smoldering wisps of a sleeping fire. Disagreements between the Croats and Muslims throughout Bosnia over elections, combining their militaries, and allocating reconstruction aid funds could stir the smoking ashes to the flash point.

Other worrisome spots

In a worst case scenario, a second Bosnian war could, indeed, erupt in Mostar or anywhere else in the strained Muslim-Croat Federation. The two groups have always distrusted one another, and the enmity created by two years as enemies cannot be expected to fade simply because they have shared a common foe since.

The Muslim city of Sarajevo could also be the place to flash if Serb snipers and bombers resume their threatened aggressions. And Iranian-inspired Bosnian Muslim terrorists could upset the teetering balance altogether by attacking any and all "infidels" as they have sworn themselves to their god to do.

IFOR soldiers patrol war-damaged areas of Mostar on January 14, 1996. Hostilities between Muslims and Croats have continued to rise in Mostar, despite the efforts of peacekeepers to forge a Muslim-Croat federation in the city.

Fighting might spark between the Bosnian Serbs and the IFOR forces as it nearly has on several occasions. Any possible attempts to capture indicted war criminals such as Karadzic and Mladic would certainly result in ground-soaking bloodshed on both sides. As recently as August 1996, a gun-pointing standoff between American IFOR troops and Bosnian Serbs protecting their mountaintop headquarters at Pale nearly resulted in combat as did an IFOR effort to locate and destroy a huge cache of illegal Serbian weapons.

But most Balkan observers agree that if war is to bare its fangs again, it will likely do so first at a crossroads town near the Serbian Republic and the Muslim-Croat Federation border in northern Bosnia: a town called Brčko. Both entities of Bosnia claim that the town belongs to them and both consider it to be strategically essential.

The Serbs say they need Brčko to guard a narrow corridor of land that connects the eastern and western parts of the Serbian Republic. The Croats and Muslims, whom the Serbs ejected from the town early in the war, insist that they need it in order to link themselves commercially to the north with Croatia, Hungary, and central Europe. The resulting stakes are high. One Muslim said, "We want to go back to our houses, but if the Serbs don't let us in, it will be war for sure." Two treaty talks have already broken down over the issue and the Dayton signatories merely postponed making a decision on who will get it.

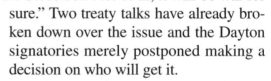

As if they needed reasons

So war could come to Brčko. Or Mostar. Or Sarajevo. Or Tuzla. It could even come from somewhere outside Bosnia altogether. It could start with tanks or artillery or rifles or rockets. It could even start with Iranian terrorist bombs. One thing is definite, however. Regardless of where the fighting would begin or how the death-dealing blows

A Serbian child carts rubble from a war-stricken section of Brčko, where observers believe feuding between the Serbian Republic and the Muslim-Croat Federation may erupt into war as both sides vie for possession of the town.

"Our peace dove should take off momentarily!"

would be delivered, there is no shortage of reasons why it might commence. There is no lack of hatreds to fuel men's passions and possess their angry souls.

The reasons might be rooted in history, religion, culture, prejudice, greed, lust, or vengeance; or love of family, hatred of those who might harm them, unbridled men turned bad, or evil ones turned even worse. Leaders might claim infractions of treaties, mismanagement of reconstruction funds, border disputes, corruption, and violations of election rules. They might simply want more land, more power, more respect, more prestige, more money, more resources, or just plain more.

There are, indeed, many reasons why the Bosnians might rise up and tear themselves apart again. But there is at least one reason why they might not. The ethnic communities of Bosnia have now experienced war firsthand and it would seem unlikely that they would want to go through those horrors again. They have killed. They have seen others killed. They have been wounded and splattered with the blood of their children. They have been shelled out of their homes and driven half-clad into the snow. They have suffered disease, starvation, torture, and rape. So why would they ever choose war over peace, especially when the rest of the world is investing so much time, effort, and money into rebuilding a peaceful nation for them?

The options

Whether the Bosnians, Croats, and Serbs go back to war or not will depend heavily upon how successful they decide that the Dayton accords have been. And there are two perspectives on assessing that. During the six months preceding the signing of the accords, the Muslims were still trying to battle their way out of Sarajevo, the Serbs were allegedly murdering thousands of Muslims near Srebrenica, and the Croats were ethnically cleansing 150,000 Serbs from their ancestral homelands. In the months following Dayton, Bosnia's problems have surrounded election fraud, the apprehension of war criminals, and providing food, shelter, and basic needs to the survivors. And while the latter troubles are certainly serious, they fall short of the direct wartime terrors that the Dayton cease-fire brought to a close. So, in that sense, Dayton has been successful.

However, the other aspect that must be considered when evaluating the success or failure of the Dayton Peace Agreement is the ultimate result it will bring to Bosnia. It is too early to say what that result will be, but there are three likely possibilities. First, the accords could be implemented as they were intended to be, creating a harmonious Bosnian nation comprised of the Muslim-Croat Federation and the Serbian Republic. Old wounds would heal and prosperity would return. Second, Bosnia could be partitioned into three separate, antagonistic states (Serbian, Croatian, and Muslim) each with hardened borders. The Bosnian Serbs would eventually fall into the economic and political sphere of Serbia proper, the Bosnian Croats would do the same with Croatia, and the Bosnian Muslims

For the Dayton Peace Agreement to succeed, the Bosnian, Serbian, and Croatian survivors must put aside vengeance in favor of peace.

would probably become an international protectorate with increasingly close ties to Iran. And third, any of a thousand potential flash points and flash circumstances could flare up into a second round of hostilities, relegating the Dayton accords to the trash heap of other failed attempts to bring peace to the Balkans and rain down the flesh-searing sulfur of war once again.

Still a tale of woe

In the final analysis, it is up to the Serbs, Croats, and Muslims to choose what they want for themselves. For only they have the power to stop or start a war. Indeed, it would be presumptuous of anyone but them to decide whether they can forget the cries of their children and bury their vengeance with their dead.

It is telling to revisit the father of "Juliet" in the opening story about the Romeo and Juliet of Sarajevo: the star-crossed Muslim girl and Serbian boy who were gunned down for their love in a bullet-raked no-man's-land. Three years after his beloved daughter's death, his grieving eyes still burning bitterly, the father vowed into a video camera, "I will get them. . . . I will get them. . . . I will get the bastards who killed my girl." And as he exhaled heavily, the blue smoke of his cigarette closed in and consumed him.

Glossary

accord: An agreement or reconciliation.

Balkans: Mountainous, peninsular region of southeast Europe including Croatia, Bosnia, and Rump Yugoslavia.

Chetniks: Serbian nationalists who fought against the German occupation troops, their Croatian allies, and Tito's Communists during World War II (1939–1945).

client states: Nations or parts of nations that are dependent upon another stronger nation for support.

Eastern Orthodox: The body of Christian churches, including the Greek, Russian, and Serbian Orthodox, derived from the Byzantine Empire.

ethnic cleansing: The forcible removal of one ethnic group by another from disputed territory.

Federation of Bosnia and Herzegovina: The entity representing the Muslim-Croat half of the proposed nation of Bosnia.

Greater Serbia: The idea that there will someday be one extended nation within which all Balkan Serbs will live, presumably on land now belonging to Croatia and Bosnia.

indictment: The formal accusation of a criminal charge.

infrastructure: The permanent installations required for the maintenance of civilization (i.e., transportation, communication, power, sanitation, etc.).

Inter-Entity Boundary Line: The demarcation within the new nation of Bosnia that separates the Serbian Republic from the Muslim-Croat Federation.

Islam: The religious faith of Muslims that professes that Allah is God and Muhammad is his only prophet.

mission creep: The drifting away from the originally stated objectives of an undertaking.

nationalism: The belief that every ethnic group should rule itself within the context of its own country.

NATO: North Atlantic Treaty Organization; international organization comprised principally of North American and European countries for purposes of defense and the promotion of common strategic interests.

paramilitaries: Armed yet untrained civilians who fight alongside regular soldiers.

Partisans: Communist Yugoslavs led by Marshal Tito who fought against German occupation troops, Croatian Ustaša, and Serbian Chetniks during World War II.

partitioning: The dividing of a formerly mixed, multiethnic nation into smaller segregated states comprised of only one ethnic group each.

patron: A larger, richer nation that helps support a smaller, poorer one.

proximity talks: Negotiations in which the competing parties are isolated from each other while remaining in the same general area so that demands and counterdemands may be exchanged by third parties thereby limiting confrontations.

Realpolitik: National and international policy that is dictated more by practical (though not always ethical) considerations rather than purely moral and idealistic ones.

reconstruction: The physical, economic, and psychological rebuilding of a devastated country.

Republika Srpska: The semiautonomous Bosnian Serb state that makes up half of the newly formed nation of Bosnia.

Roman Catholicism: The religious faith that professes that God is made up of three distinct persons, the Father, his only Son (Jesus Christ), and the Holy Spirit. Roman Catholics regard the pope in Rome as the infallible interpreter of revealed truth.

Rump Yugoslavia: What remains of the original Yugoslavia after its breakup, including Serbia, Montenegro, and the semiautonomous provinces of Kosovo and Vojvodina.

safe areas: Cities such as Goražde, Zepa, and Srebrenica guarded by UN troops and designed to protect Muslim refugees.

sanctions: A penalty used to enforce compliance or conformity.

self-determination: The exercise of a group's authority to rule themselves.

semiautonomous state: A partially independent province ultimately under the authority of a larger, more powerful state.

signatories: The signers of an agreement.

tribunal: A seat or court of justice originally made up of three judges.

Ustaša: Croatians who sympathized and collaborated with the occupying forces of Nazi Germany during World War II.

Suggestions for Further Reading

Yossef Bodansky, *Offensive in the Balkans.* Alexandria, VA: International Strategic Studies Association, 1995.

Arthur L. Clark, *Bosnia: What Every American Should Know.* New York: Berkley Books, 1996.

Zlatko Dizdarevic, *Sarajevo: A War Journal.* New York: Fromm International, 1993.

Zlata Filipovic, *Zlata's Dairy.* New York: Viking Press, 1994.

Edward R. Ricciuti, *War in Yugoslavia.* Brookfield, CT: Millbrook Press, 1993.

Laura Silber and Allan Little, *Yugoslavia: Death of a Nation.* New York: T.V. Books, 1996.

Bob Stewart, *Broken Lives: A Personal View of the Balkan Conflict.* London: HarperCollins, 1993.

Additional Works Consulted

Fouad Ajami, "Why Bosnia Needs a Nuremberg," *U.S. News & World Report*, February 19, 1996.

"All Agree Karadzic Is Out, Not Down," Associated Press, July 22, 1996.

Mark Almond, *Europe's Backyard War.* London: Mandarin, 1994.

Jim Bartlett, "Future Looks Bleak for Young Workers in Sarajevo," Beserkistan, BosNet, July 18, 1996.

Jim Bartlett, "Sarajevo's Terminator," Beserkistan, BosNet, March 13, 1996.

Jim Bartlett, "Veterinarians Sans Frontiers Needed by Bosnia's Horses," Beserkistan, BosNet, June 2, 1996.

Sharon Begley, "The Dead Tell Tales," *Time*, April 15, 1996.

Carl Bildt, "Bosnia's Shaky Truce," *The Times* (London), June 13, 1996.

"Blaskic: 'Completely Innocent,'" Beserkistan in Bosnia, BosNet, April 17, 1996.

"Bosnia Mass Grave May Be Near U.S. Army Base," Reuters, Nando.net, January 28, 1996.

"Bosnian Atrocities Revealed—1,000 Exterminated," Reuters, March 23, 1996.

"Bosnian Serbs Bow to NATO Pressure," Reuters, August 12, 1996.

Bosnia Peace Agreement, U.S. State Department, March 1, 1996.

"Bosnia Progress Slow, Admiral Says," *Dallas Morning News*, June 8, 1996.

"Burnout in Bosnia," Beserkistan, BosNet, January 27, 1996.

"Canadian IFOR Troops Accused of Beatings, Sex, in Bosnian Mental Hospital," Beserkistan in Bosnia, Alta Vista Internet, July 17, 1996.

"Chief Prosecutor Vows to Go after Anyone Implicated by Evidence," Associated Press, Nando.net, January 28, 1996.

George Church, "In Harm's Way," *Time*, December 25, 1995.

Norman Cigar, *Genocide in Bosnia.* College Station: Texas A & M University Press, 1995.

Paul W. Cockerham, "The Bosnian Chronicles: A Day-by-Day Account," Part 1, *Military Technical Journal*, June 1996.

Paul W. Cockerham, "The Bosnian Chronicles: A Day-by-Day Account," Part 2, *Military Technical Journal,* August 1996.

"Controversy Surrounds Moslems Handed Over to Serbs," Reuters, May 13, 1996.

"Croatia Charges Journalists with Libeling President Tudjman," Reuters, May 4, 1996.

"Croats, Muslims Agree to Joint Government for Mostar," Associated Press, August 7, 1996.

"The Dead Cry Out," *Newsweek*, February 5, 1996.

Vladimir Dedijer, *The Yugoslav Auschwitz and the Vatican.* Buffalo, NY: Prometheus Books, 1992.

Dan DeLuce, "Tomorrow's Geneva Summit: Assuring Bosnia's Elections," Reuters, June 1, 1996.

Barbara Demic, "Karadzic Gives Up His Duties; Balks at Quitting Bosnia Post," Knight-Ridder News Service, July 1, 1996.

Gwynne Dyer, "Appeasement: Karadzic Dupes UN Mediator—Twice," *San Diego Union-Tribune,* July 17, 1996.

"Envoy to Warn Serbs About Possibility of New Sanctions," *New York Times*, July 12, 1996.

"EU Considers Mostar Withdrawal," Associated Press, August 5, 1996.

"Evidence Points to a Civilian Massacre in Bosnia," *USA Today*, July 12, 1996.

William Finnegan, "Salt City: Letters from Tuzla," *New Yorker*, February 12, 1996.

"Forces of Partition Intensify," This Week in Bosnia-Herzegovina, BosNet, August 19, 1996.

Alain Franchon, "The U.S. Ruffles Gallic Feathers," *Le Monde* (Paris), November 29, 1995.

"Fugitive Serb Ready to Confront Tribunal," *New York Times*, July 11, 1996.

"GAO Finds New Costs in Bosnian Mission," Associated Press, August 7, 1996.

"Getting the Job Done," *Newsweek*, January 15, 1996.

Misha Glenny, *The Fall of Yugoslavia.* New York: Penguin, 1992.

"Gore: U.S. Troops Out of Bosnia by Year's End," Associated Press, July 22, 1996.

Roy Gutmann, *Witness to Genocide*. New York: MacMillan, 1993.

David H. Hackworth, "The Guy in Charge," *Newsweek*, January 15, 1996.

Chris Hedges, "Swiss Diplomat Resists U.S. on Certifying Bosnian Vote," *New York Times*, June 7, 1996.

Helsinki Human Rights Watch, "Major War Criminals/Suspects," July 27, 1996.

Michael Hirsh, "Back to the Woodshed," *Newsweek*, February 26, 1996.

Richard Holbrooke, "Backsliding in Bosnia," *Time*, May 26, 1996.

Davor Huic, "Croatian Police Arrest War Crimes Suspect," Reuters, June 9, 1996.

"In Focus: Bosnia," *National Geographic*, June 1996.

"In Hot Pursuit of War Criminals," *Newsweek*, February 19, 1996.

"Investigators Unearth Grisly Find in Srebrenica," Associated Press, July 25, 1996.

Greg Ip, "Trying to Make Peace Pay," *Globe and Mail* (Toronto), July 1, 1996.

James O. Jackson, "The Crimes of Croatia," *Time*, March 11, 1996.

Robert D. Kaplan, *Balkan Ghosts: A Journey Through History*. New York: St. Martin's Press, 1993.

"Karadzic's Intentions Matter of Speculation," Associated Press, July 3, 1996.

Michael Kelly, "The Negotiator," *New Yorker*, November 6, 1995.

Jovan Kovacic, "Bildt: Patience and Persistence Are Keys to Peace in Bosnia," Reuters, June 10, 1996.

Jovan Kovacic, "Tribunal Chief to Request Sanction Against Serbs," Reuters, June 6, 1996.

Samir Krilic, "Serb Leader Gives Up Post," Associated Press, June 18, 1996.

"Lacking Capital, Small Business Finds It Tough Going in Sarajevo," Beserkistan, BosNet, July 7, 1996.

Jane Laing, ed., *Chronicle of the Year 1995*. London: Dorling-Kindersley Books, 1996.

"Let's Get Out of Here," *Newsweek*, June 26, 1995.

Florence Levinsohn, *Belgrade: Among the Serbs.* Chicago: I. R. Dee, 1994.

Finlay Lewis, "Summit Leaders Caution Serbia," Copley News Service, June 30, 1996.

Melinda Liu and Christopher Dickey, "The Arms Dealer," *Newsweek*, June 3, 1996.

Peter Maas, *Love Thy Neighbor: A Story of War.* New York: Alfred A. Knopf, 1996.

Branka Magos, *The Destruction of Yugoslavia.* London: Verso, 1993.

"Mass Grave Exhumed," United Press, June 25, 1996.

"Mass Grave in Bosnia Produces Poignant Evidence," Associated Press, July 18, 1996.

Joanna McGeary, "Face to Face with Evil," *Time*, May 13, 1996.

Mark Milstein, "Sarajevo 'Olympics': Pillage, Rape, Burn, and Bug-Out," *Soldier of Fortune*, July 1996.

"A Muslim Family Saved by Serbs," *Time*, April 1, 1996.

"NATO Admonishes Serbs to Honor Accord," *USA Today*, August 13, 1996.

"NATO Pilots Still Facing Threats," Air Force News Service, August 7, 1996.

Bruce W. Nelan, "Now It's Serb Against Serb," *Time*, January 22, 1996.

Bruce W. Nelan, "Seeds of Evil," *Time*, July 29, 1996.

Bruce W. Nelan, "Tears and Terror," *Time*, July 24, 1995.

Bruce W. Nelan, "War on All Fronts," *Time*, August 7, 1995.

Rob Norland, "Death of a Village," *Time*, April 15, 1996.

Rob Norland, "A Monster on the Loose," *Newsweek*, April 22, 1996.

Mike O'Conner, "Attacks on Foreigners in Bosnia Boost Tensions, NATO Concerns," *New York Times*, July 14, 1996.

"Officials Visit Atrocity Sites, See Only Fresh Paint," Associated Press, Nando.net, February 6, 1996.

"Only One of 52 Indicted by War Crimes Tribunal in Custody," Associated Press, February 6, 1996.

David Owen, *Balkan Odyssey*. New York: Harcourt Brace and Company, 1995.

Edmond Paris, *Genocide in Satellite Croatia*. Chicago: American Institute for Balkan Affairs, 1961.

"Pentagon Changing Troop Makeup in Bosnia," *USA Today*, July 4, 1996.

"Perry: U.S. Has 'Important Clues' in Graves Probe," Associated Press, February 14, 1996.

"Perspectives on Bosnia: Europe Can't Shake Its Dependence on U.S.," *Los Angeles Times*, April 6, 1996.

"Poll Serbs, Croats Oppose Unified Bosnia," Reuters, August 8, 1996.

John Ponfret, "An Atrocity the Serbs Didn't Commit," *Sacramento Bee*, August 21, 1994.

"Reconstruction of Bosnia and Herzegovina," World Bank Home Page, last updated August 6, 1996.

"Red Cross Finds 88 Serb Prisoners in Bosnian Jail," Reuters, Nando.net, February 2, 1996.

"Same Land, Same Fate," *Time*, August 28, 1996.

Tim Sebastion, "A Willfully Blind Eye in the Sky," *The Mail* (London), February 24, 1996.

"Serbs Decry Arrests of Suspected War Criminals," *New York Times*, February 6, 1996.

"Serb Women Hold Senior Diplomats," Associated Press, June 19, 1996.

Arnold Sherman, *Perfidy in the Balkans: The Rape of Yugoslavia*. Athens: Psigogios Publications, 1993.

Michael Shields, "Milosevic Questions Tribunal's Impartiality," Reuters, Beserkistan Internet, June 8, 1996.

Ann Simmons, "War Welcome, Cold Feet," *Time*, January 13, 1996.

Susan Sontag, "A Lament for Bosnia," *Nation,* April 1996.

Barry Sweid, "Talks on Serb War Criminals to Begin," Associated Press, July 15, 1996.

"Team Unearths Bodies in Killing Field," *New York Times*, July 10, 1996.

"Text of the General Framework Agreement for Peace in Bosnia and Herzegovina," December 5, 1995.

"Three Bosnian Croats Arrested in Shooting of U.S. Diplomat," Reuters, July 24, 1996.

Mark Thompson, "Generals for Hire," *Time*, January 15, 1996.

Mark Thompson, *A Paper House: The Ending of Yugoslavia*. New York: Pantheon Books, 1992.

"Tribunal Indicts 8 Bosnian Serbs for Organized Rape," Associated Press, June 28, 1996.

"Troops Want Their Beer, Flag, and Leave Time," *USA Today*, March 20, 1996.

"Two Elderly Serbs Found Killed in Recaptured Area," Associated Press, Nando.net, February 6, 1996.

"2 French Troops Die, 9 Injured in Bosnia," Associated Press, June 29, 1996.

"The Unseen Killers," *Time*, February 12, 1996.

"UN War Crimes Tribunal Charges First Muslims," Reuters, Nando.net, March 23, 1996.

"UN War Crimes Tribunal Issues Warrants for Karadzic, Mladic," Associated Press, July 12, 1996.

"U.S. Allies May Back Selective Serbian Sanctions," Reuters, June 19, 1996.

"U.S. Ends Yugoslavia Arms Embargo," Associated Press, June 19, 1996.

"U.S. Official Warns Slow Bosnia Recovery Could Be Fatal," Associated Press, March 26, 1996.

"U.S. Soldiers Flee Mladic Encounter," This Week in Bosnia-Herzegovina, BosNet, August 19, 1996.

"U.S. Troops Confront Serb Tanks, Armor," Associated Press, July 7, 1996.

"U.S. Troops Meet Hostility at Serb Hideout," Associated Press, July 7, 1996.

Martin Van Heuven, "Understanding the Balkan Breakup," *Foreign Policy,* summer 1996.

James Walsh, "Unearthing Evil," *Time*, January 29, 1996.

"War-Scarred Olympic Stadium Brought Back to Life," *USA Today*, August 20, 1996.

"Weapons for Bosnian Army Delivered," Associated Press, July 23, 1996.

"Western Mediator Says Gangsters Behind Croat Boycott," Reuters, July 28, 1996.

"Will Justice Be Done?," *U.S. News & World Report*, December 25, 1996.

Susan L. Woodward, *Balkan Tragedy: Chaos and Dissolution After the Cold War*. Washington, DC: The Brookings Institution, 1996.

John Zaritsky, *Romeo and Juliet in Sarajevo* (video recording), New York: Public Broadcasting System, 1993.

Warren Zimmerman, "The Last Ambassador," *Foreign Affairs*, March/April 1995.

Index

About the Author

James P. Reger's passion for international politics and military history stretches far back into his childhood when his parents shared their ardent interest in world affairs and encouraged discussions of them around the dinner table. Civil wars have especially compelled him with their bitter love-hate poignance and their doubly destructive effects on the victim nations. Hailing from West Virginia, he claims many relatives and ancestors who experienced the particularly cruel results of the American Civil War and he knows first-hand the generational residue from those ancient divisions that lingers yet today.

Mr. Reger graduated from West Virginia University after studying history, psychology, English, and political science. He presently teaches school in San Diego, California. He has written two other works for Lucent Books, *The Battle of Antietam* and *Life in the South During the Civil War*. When not writing, he enjoys spending time with his wife and young son.

Picture Credits
